MINDFUL MOMENTS
FOR BUSY MOTHERS

MINDFUL MOMENTS
FOR BUSY MOTHERS

DAILY MEDITATIONS AND MANTRAS FOR GREATER CALM, BALANCE AND JOY

SARAH RUDELL BEACH

CICO BOOKS

LONDON NEW YORK

FOR *Abby*
AND *Liam*

I LOVE YOU TO THE MOON
AND BACK, AND I LOVE
BEING YOUR MOM.

Published in 2018 by CICO Books
An imprint of Ryland Peters & Small Ltd
20–21 Jockey's Fields   341 E 116th St
London WC1R 4BW   New York, NY 10029

www.rylandpeters.com

10 9 8 7 6 5 4 3 2 1

A CIP catalog record for this book is available from the
Library of Congress and the British Library.

US ISBN: 978-1-78249-651-9
UK ISBN: 978-1-78249-612-0

Printed in China

Editor: Dawn Bates
Designer: Abi Read
Illustrator: Clare Nicholas

Commissioning editor: Kristine Pidkameny
Senior editor: Carmel Edmonds
Art director: Sally Powell
Head of production: Patricia Harrington
Publishing manager: Penny Craig
Publisher: Cindy Richards

Contents

Introduction

Being a mother is amazing—and it's also really hard.

Some days, you can barely contain your joy. On other days, you can barely handle your frustration and exhaustion. Some days, your children are absolutely delightful and on other days, they drive you absolutely crazy!

To borrow the title of mindfulness expert Jon Kabat-Zinn's bestselling book about mindfulness, motherhood truly is "the full catastrophe." Motherhood is blissful and boring, exciting and excruciating, exhilarating and exhausting, and everything in between. Our task as mothers is to find a way to be in the center of it all, without losing our cool, or ourselves, along the way.

As a mother, you've heard the advice about putting on your own oxygen mask before assisting your children and how you can't pour from an empty cup. You hear all these maxims because they're true. The problem is that a lot of the self-care advice out there for mothers focuses on "quick fixes," or you're told to "just treat yourself" to a massage and a pedicure once in a while.

But as a busy mother, you need something that goes deeper than that. You need something that works on a *soul* level, a practice that can be woven into your days, and transforms how you approach all the parts of your life, including motherhood.

That's where mindfulness comes in.

Mindfulness seems to be everywhere now,

and you probably already know that being "present" and "peaceful" would be really good for your emotional health (hey, you're reading this book, after all!) But a lot of the time, despite your best intentions to bring a calm and compassionate awareness to the act of mothering, you often do the opposite: you end up overreacting, yelling, issuing threats, stressing out, and feeling defeated and depleted.

I know this because I've been there.

I came to the practice of mindfulness over a decade ago, as a new mother struggling with postpartum depression. I had desperately wanted to be a mother, and was completely in love with my daughter, but I was miserable. Motherhood challenged me and made me feel incompetent in ways I had never experienced before. When I finally summoned the courage to ask for help, I was introduced to mindfulness.

I was pretty sure right off the bat that mindfulness would *not* work for me. I assumed it was some kind of New Age, woo-woo, hippy fad that would never fit into my suburban working life. When I went home and did some Googling, the images of serenely smiling Buddha-mamas that popped up depicted a version of motherhood that I just didn't think was possible for me.

But I wanted to get better, so I gave mindfulness a try. I sat down on a pillow on my bedroom floor, closed my eyes, and "watched my breath" (which I thought was a goofy instruction since my eyes were closed). It felt a little weird, but I stayed on that pillow, allowing my body to soften as I tried to release all the holding and bracing I had been doing for so many years. I found that as my body became still and relaxed, so did my mind.

I continued to practice a little bit each day. And I can honestly tell you that *it changed my life*. Not all at once, of course, but slowly and surely, I could see a transformation. I learned more effective ways of working with my thoughts and my anxiety. I had much more peaceful interactions with my children, and my husband, and even the checkout people at the grocery store.

One day, many months later, I realized that I was smiling and laughing more than I had done before. My life hadn't gotten any funnier—I was simply able to meet the challenge and overwhelm of motherhood with greater confidence and ease. I found a peace and calm and joy within me that had been hiding for quite a while.

Mindfulness gave me such a gift that I began to pursue an entirely new career direction, as I transitioned from being a high-school history teacher to becoming a full-time mindfulness instructor. I now spend my days teaching mindfulness to mothers, children, teachers, students, and now, **YOU**.

WHAT IS MINDFULNESS AND WHY DO MOTHERS NEED IT?

Mindfulness is purposeful awareness of the present moment. With mindfulness, we accept what is happening right now, with curiosity and without judgment. Mindfulness means we know what we are thinking when we are thinking it, and what we are feeling when we're feeling it. It gives us the ability to pause, and to respond skillfully to challenges, instead of reacting based on our unconscious habits. Mindfulness brings us into the only moment we have—*now*—and allows us to see the goodness (or even just the okayness) that is present even in the most ordinary of experiences.

WHY DO MOTHERS NEED MINDFULNESS?

Neuroscientist Rick Hanson has recently suggested that mothers in the developed world are suffering from what he calls Depleted Mom Syndrome. Mothers still carry the work of the so-called "second shift," are sleep- and exercise-deprived, and, according to Hanson, we suffer from "guilt, anxiety, conflicting role expectations ... mood swings, irritability, [and] hopelessness."

The mothers I work with are overwhelmed, stressed out, distracted, busy, overscheduled, and rushing through their days, with a sense that they are missing out on their own lives.

Hanson and other psychologists agree: what mothers need is self-care, emotional awareness and acceptance, and greater presence and well-being.

Mindfulness is the most powerful tool I know of for helping mothers do *all* of that. Mindfulness helps us regulate our emotional responses and soothe our overtaxed nervous systems. It allows us to find a place of peace and stability within our own bodies, so we can experience nourishing self-care when and where we need it, not just at the spa. Mindfulness helps us keep our cool when our children are fired up, and, I can tell you from my own personal experience, keeps us from losing our ... *ahem*, **stuff** every day.

WHAT IT LOOKS LIKE WHEN MOTHERS PRACTICE MINDFULNESS

Let's break down that definition of mindfulness:

PURPOSEFUL AWARENESS OF THE PRESENT MOMENT

Sometimes we're paying attention, but not on purpose. It's the honk of another car, or a child yelling for attention the tenth time that day that jolts us out of our distraction. Mindfulness is paying attention *on purpose*. Mindfulness is an intentional awareness of the sensations, thoughts, feelings, and experiences of the present moment.

We spend a lot of our time thinking about the past or planning for the future. When we are mindful, we are paying attention to our present moment experience. For example, if you serve dinner and your child immediately responds with, "But I *hate* chicken," you would pay attention to your body's response—your racing pulse, your clenched jaw, the anger rising in your chest. You wouldn't *stop* all those responses, you would simply become *aware* of them. But instead of letting that anger lead to a long-winded speech about your continuous acts of sacrifice for your family, mindfulness would help you …

ACCEPT WHAT IS HAPPENING RIGHT NOW, WITH CURIOSITY AND WITHOUT JUDGMENT

You would allow the present moment to be what it is … because it's already here and happening. You wouldn't have to *like* the present moment—you can find it pretty unpleasant to cook your famous chicken parmesan only to have your child complain about it—but you wouldn't fight that it's actually happening. Instead, you'd accept it without judgment, and get curious: Why is my child getting upset? Did something happen today? Why am I getting so upset about the fact that she's getting upset? Did something happen today?

When I first started practicing mindfulness, I thought not judging things meant I had to *like* everything in every moment and think that everything that happened was amazing and wonderful. *The butterflies and rainbows and whining and tantrums and potty-training—they're all beautiful! I'm so Zen!* Not only is that a totally impractical way to live your life, it's also a bit creepy.

Mindfulness is about being with the entire range of our human experience, whether it is pleasant or unpleasant.

So once you've noticed what's happening, gotten curious about it, and accepted it without judgment, you would …

KNOW WHAT YOU ARE THINKING AND WHAT YOU ARE FEELING

You would notice your thoughts of "I worked *all day long* and came home to slave over dinner for the *entire family*, and this is how I am thanked?!" You would recognize the feelings of anger, resentment, and righteous indignation. You wouldn't fight these thoughts and feelings, you'd just observe them, watching them increase in intensity and then, most likely, subside. Then you would …

PAUSE AND RESPOND SKILLFULLY, INSTEAD OF REACTING BASED ON YOUR UNCONSCIOUS HABITS

You would pause and breathe and instead of falling into your default mode (an epic sermon about your mama-martyrdom), you would lovingly remind your child of the last time she ate this meal and how much she enjoyed it. Or you might offer her the choice of what will be for dinner tomorrow night. Or you might do something else appropriate that's skillful and doesn't make the situation worse.

It's not a huge parenting victory, but it feels amazing. And, really, it *is* kind of a huge deal, because what often drains us are the small battles and frustrations and indignities throughout the day.

With mindfulness, you can discover the possibility of being a no-drama mama (or at least a low-drama mama).

SO HOW CAN YOU LEARN TO DO THIS?

One of the most important things about mindfulness is that it is a *practice*. It's something we must cultivate—we can't just read a book, decide to appreciate mindfulness and peacefulness and attentiveness from now on, and expect things to change, any more than we can read a book about exercise, decide to *appreciate* sweat and movement, and then expect to be fitter.

We have to practice. Mindfulness is like a muscle, something that will grow stronger the more we use it. The more we practice pausing, the better we will get at it. The more we practice being fully present with our breath, the better we will become at being fully present with our children. The more aware we become of the patterns of our thoughts, the less we'll be driven by them, and we'll be able to change those of our reactive habits that aren't serving us very well. And, according to the research, we'll experience less stress and greater joy. All of these things can help you enjoy motherhood more, and help you be the mother you want to be.

I like to think of our work as that of mindful *motherhood*, not mindful *parenting*. The "-ing" in mindful parenting connotes a doing, a technique, a set of strategies for how we should parent. Mindful motherhood is about internal work. It's about cultivating balance and ease; it's about resourcing ourselves before we nourish others. It's about showing up each day with presence and compassion. If today you take care to practice mindful motherhood, the mindful parenting will take care of itself.

AND HOW DO YOU FIND THE TIME?

When you're really busy, you might think taking 5 minutes to meditate just isn't worth it, because then you'll be even more behind schedule. But we often "earn back" the time we spend in mindfulness practice. Spending a few minutes in quiet stillness creates a calm and focus that will help you be more productive and efficient throughout your day.

A famous Zen saying tells us that if we don't have 1 hour for meditation in our day, then we need at least 2. I don't know *any* mother who has 2 hours for daily meditation, but I'm pretty sure you have 5 minutes! (And if you don't have 5, you probably need 10.) With mindfulness, consistency of practice is far more important than the duration of your practice. Even 5 minutes a day of breathing in attentive silence will help you cultivate greater calm, focus, and patience.

Although it's important to create time for your mindfulness practice in your day, it's also important not to make mindfulness just another item on your to-do list, a chore that must be completed. Mindfulness should be a "get to," not a "have to." Think of ways that you can ritualize your practice—maybe lighting a candle or listening to soothing music—so that your time feels special and set apart from the rest of your day. Allow your time for mindfulness to be a gift you give yourself. You are fully *on* for most of your day—taking in information,

responding to the world, moving through space, navigating your surroundings—and all that time being *on* takes its toll on your energy, clarity, and presence. Think of meditation as your time *not* to be on—not to have to respond, engage, or move. To simply *be*.

HOW TO USE THIS BOOK

This book is intended to provide both guidance and inspiration for your mindfulness practice. You'll discover lots of different ways to bring mindfulness into your busy-mama days. Think of this book as a menu, not an all-you-can-eat buffet. Sample the exercises that appeal to you, experiment with them in the laboratory of your own life, and see what works for you. If a particular practice brings you some ease and comfort, you can come back for seconds.

Honor your own feelings and intuition—if a particular mantra or meditation practice doesn't feel right to you, feel free to modify it or not do it at all. You can't do all of them every day, nor should you even try!

See if you can approach mindfulness with an attitude of playfulness—play with these practices, see what resonates with you, and consider how you can integrate mindfulness into your life as an important component of your self-care.

If you're new to mindfulness, I recommend you start with Chapter 1, as it contains many introductory practices and meditations to get you started on the basics.

Feel free to skip around in the book—when you're having a rough day, head straight to Chapter 5 for some supportive practices for the difficult moments of motherhood. If you're looking for some ways to practice mindfulness with your children, check out Chapter 6.

You could decide to try a different meditation or mantra each day for an entire year (and wouldn't you know, you've got exactly 365 of them here!). Or you could read the whole book straight through and compile your own mindfulness menu. It's entirely up to you.

Finally, I want to end by stating, as my friend and fellow mindfulness teacher Carla Naumburg once quipped, that I am not the Dalai Mama. I am not perfect, my children are not perfect, and I sometimes lose it. I am a completely human mother, who makes mistakes and makes amends. But I've practiced and studied mindfulness for years, and it's given me a way to approach motherhood, and my life, that brings me greater joy and ease than I knew before. I truly believe that if we can learn to hold ourselves, and our children, with compassionate awareness, we will change the world. This is the gift I hope to offer you, and your children, with this book.

A FEW NOTES ABOUT THE MANTRAS AND MEDITATIONS

1. I am often asked how we should breathe in meditation. Open mouth or closed mouth? In through the nose or out through the nose? The simple answer is just to let your breath be natural. You don't need to try to breathe in any particular way—in fact, trying to force the breath to be a certain way can create more stress and agitation! Simply focus on what *your* breath is like, in *your* body, right now. Breathe in the way that is most comfortable for you.

2. Some meditations begin with an instruction to "Close your eyes …" Read the meditation a few times, and *then* close your eyes and practice. You could also have someone read them to you, or you could dictate them into your phone and use the recording to practice.

3. This is a book about mindfulness and meditation. What's the difference? Mindfulness is a broad term, referring to our ability to attend to the present moment no matter what we are doing. It is something we can cultivate throughout our day, even as we engage in other activities. When I use the word "meditation," I am referring to the formal practice in which we sit (or lie) down, close our eyes, and deliberately bring our attention to a particular aspect of our experience (the breath, for example). Think of meditation sessions as the formal training you do for a few minutes every day to strengthen your mindfulness muscles. The more you practice meditation, the more you will notice an improvement in your ability to be mindful throughout your day.

4. If you fall asleep during your meditation time, that's okay. It's just a nap. And if you fell asleep that quickly, you probably needed a nap far more than you needed meditation. You can do things such as adjusting your posture and choosing a time of day to practice when you'll be most alert, but it's also totally fine to be so present with your sleepiness that you fall asleep.

5. You may think you are "bad" at mindfulness and meditation because your mind wanders a lot and keeps doing all this *thinking* when you're trying to be mindful. But when you notice that your mind has wandered away from the present moment, that's actually great news! It means you are becoming more aware of the activity of your mind—it wandered, and you noticed. That means you're absolutely doing it right.

6. The mantras throughout this book can be used in a variety of ways. You can silently repeat them in your head a few times during your formal practice, or whenever you need them throughout the day. You could even say them out loud if you find it helpful. Once you discover the mantras that most resonate with you, you could write them down on a post-it, or perhaps even on your favorite stationery, and fix them where you will see them during the day (on your mirror, on the refrigerator, etc.).

CHAPTER 1

Begin

MINDFULNESS PRACTICES

The meditations and mantras in this chapter will help you to ease into a mindfulness practice. You can use these exercises "on the go" as you need them, or you can make them part of a formal mindfulness time each day. By taking small steps, you will gradually cultivate greater awareness, presence, and calm. Try to spend 5–10 minutes every day experimenting with different exercises. You'll soon discover the ones that work most effectively for you and help you approach the challenging work of motherhood with greater ease.

FIVE SENSES
Meditation

Close your eyes, and identify one thing you can notice, right at this moment, with each of your five senses. What do you smell? What sounds do you hear? Where is your body making contact with the world? What do you see? Can you taste anything? Your awareness of your sensory experiences brings you directly into the present moment.

KEEP AN Open Mind

Try to approach your practice without any preconceived ideas of how it's supposed to look or feel or be. You may find that your practice is relaxing, but that isn't the "goal." One day it might be relaxing. The next day it might be boring. And then the next day you just feel hungry and your back hurts. And then the day after that, you love it. Just notice whatever is happening when you practice— if you hate it, notice that you're hating it. If you are tense and irritated, notice that you are tense and irritated. If you think you are really bad at mindfulness, notice that you are thinking you are bad at mindfulness!

Scan YOUR BODY

Close your eyes, and as you breathe, gently scan your body. See if you can identify somewhere in your body that feels pleasant, perhaps a sense of relaxation in the face, or warmth in the hands. Spend some time with this sensation. How do you know it is pleasant? What is pleasant about it? How does it feel to spend time focusing on a part of the body that feels good?

Then do the same thing with an unpleasant sensation: what is it, how do you know it's unpleasant, and what happens when you bring awareness to it? There's no "right" or "wrong" way to do this meditation, but you might notice that 1) you have some choice in where you place your attention, and 2) what you pay attention to can impact your present moment experience.

A *Short* AND *Sweet* SIMPLE MEDITATION

Meditation does not need to be mysterious, complicated, or time-consuming. Set a timer for 5 minutes, and allow your eyes to close. Now count your breaths—begin counting "1" on the inhale, then "2" on the exhale, and so on, until you reach 10, and then start over again at 1. If your mind wanders away from counting your breath (which it will most likely do), just start over again at 1. You may start over 73 times in 5 minutes, and that's okay. Just continue focusing on your breath until the timer goes off, and then see how you feel when you're done!

MANTRA

WITH EACH BREATH
I RELEASE TENSION.

TAKE
Three Breaths

No matter how busy your day is, you have time to pause for three deep breaths. You don't even need to close your eyes. Wherever you are, you can stop for a moment and bring your attention to your breath. On the first breath, focus on what it feels like as you inhale, as you bring nourishing oxygen to your body. On the second breath, focus on the exhale, and enjoy the soothing effects of the out-breath. On the third breath, breathe in what you need—perhaps love, energy, and wisdom—and release any feelings you don't need—perhaps resentment, worry, and anger.

Relax YOUR FACE

This simple exercise will help you to become mindful of any tension you hold in your face and help you relax. Take a deep breath, and bring your awareness to your face. Unclench your teeth, and allow your jaw to relax or even drop open. Soften the muscles around your mouth. Release any holding in your cheeks. Soften your eyes; unfurrow your brow. Feel your breath gently entering your nose, and then gliding over your lips as you exhale. Allow your entire face to be soft and at rest.

"I AM *Aware* AND IN THE *Moment*"

Awareness, as hard as it can be to cultivate sometimes, is actually your natural state. With mindfulness, you're not trying to manufacture some extra-ordinary blissful experience; you're simply resting in the awareness that is always available to you, in any moment. You can be aware of your child sitting next to you. You can be aware of your child's voice, the story she's telling you, and the expressions on her face. This, too, is mindfulness. Repeat the mantra "I Am Aware and In the Moment."

FIND YOUR *Anchor*

A helpful way to begin mindfulness meditation is to identify an anchor that you can bring your attention to. This can be your breath, the sensations in your body, or the sounds in your environment. It doesn't really matter which anchor you choose—it's simply there to provide your busy mind with a place to return to when it wanders. Just like a boat might drift away a bit before being gently tugged back into place, your mind will float along on a thought until your anchor brings you back to the present moment. For the next few moments, choose an anchor for your attention, such as your breath, a part of your body, or a sound, and close your eyes. When your mind wanders, keep coming back to your anchor. Again and again.

Tune In TO YOUR BREATH

All day long, your body performs the miraculous task of keeping you alive, with no real involvement on your part. Your lungs breathe, your stomach digests, your heart beats, and your neurons fire. So when you practice mindfulness, you don't need to bring a lot of extra effort to it. You don't have to force the breath—just let the body breathe, and pay attention.

Notice JUDGMENTS

The primary task of your brain is to keep you alive, so it spends much of its time judging things: "Is this okay? Am I safe? Should I approach or avoid?" Most of the time, you don't even know this is happening … and this is where you can get into trouble. Your mind starts judging a situation, and before you even realize what's happened, you've jumped to all sorts of (likely inaccurate) conclusions about it. For today, see if you can notice all the times you are judging things ("I like this, I don't like that"), and see what impact those judgments have on your experience.

BE IN
This Moment

It's so easy for our thoughts to get pulled into the future or stuck in the past. When you notice your thoughts racing forward to the next moment, or dwelling on some previous moment, see if you can bring yourself to *this* moment. Right here, right now. What is happening now? What is needed of you *now*?

MANTRA

I CAN

BE

HERE

NOW.

FIND THE *Roots* OF THE *Tree*

We often refer to our minds as "monkey minds," because they jump from thought to thought as often as monkeys leap from branch to branch. As you practice mindfulness, you'll start to get familiar with the branches your monkey mind likes to swing around on. You might notice the same thought patterns and worries appear again and again in meditation. I like to think of this as finally starting to see the *roots* of the tree your monkey mind keeps circling. And once you've identified those roots, you've discovered some helpful information! Perhaps a thought keeps popping up because there's something you need to resolve. Noticing these repetitive thought patterns is not a problem in meditation—it's the beginning of insight.

PRACTICE WHEN IT'S *Easy*

Some days, spending 10 minutes (or even 5 minutes!) just breathing might seem like a complete waste of time. You can probably think of about 18 other things you could be doing during those 10 minutes. But that time of breathing … resting … stopping … settling … calming … is actually time incredibly well spent. If you practice mindfulness when it's easy, you'll be able to do it when it's hard. When you hit a tough moment in your day, you'll know how to pause and calm yourself down. When it gets hard, you'll know what to do.

Ask, "WHAT IS THIS?"

You can ask this question at any moment of your day. What is this? "Ah, this is anger …" "Ah, this is an overtired child." "Ah, this is resentment." Mindfulness is simply about clearly knowing what *this* is.

MANTRA

I WILL FOCUS ON WHAT I CAN CONTROL.

KNOW THAT IT'S JUST *This*

Whatever you're doing, just do it, and know that you are doing it. Mindfulness is knowing you're …
Just cleaning
Just driving
Just rocking
Just playing
Just eating
Just singing
Just cooking
Just walking
Just coloring
Just talking
Just sitting
Just reading
Just being

See the World AS YOUR CHILD SEES THE WORLD

Our children approach the world with a true beginner's mind—everything is new to them! They are fascinated by things such as onions, insects, leaves, belly buttons, water bottles, and faces. They truly *see* what they are looking at, with curiosity and delight. What would it be like if *you* looked at the world this way today?

MANTRA

PEACE IS AVAILABLE TO ME
IN EVERY MOMENT OF THE DAY.

Check
YOUR REACTIONS

Every feeling you have fundamentally boils down to the question of whether you are drawn to approach or avoid something. Today, set an intention to notice your immediate reactions to the events of your day. Notice if there is a visceral sense of pleasantness or unpleasantness, and if this instant assessment begins to impact the thoughts you are having about what's happening. You don't need to get upset with yourself for reacting to things so quickly—it's what your body was designed to do. But see if you can notice how these immediate feelings of attraction or revulsion impact your mood, and your behavior.

Check It Out

This is a helpful mantra to remind yourself to check in with yourself throughout your day. Just tell yourself to "check it out": where are you, what are you doing, what are you thinking, how are you feeling? Just be present for a moment, and check it out.

Listen
MINDFULLY

Close your eyes, and just listen. You don't have to "work hard" at hearing—just allow the sounds in your environment to come to you. Can you hear any sounds from within your body? Do you hear your breath? What can you hear in this room? Outside this room? If you don't really notice any sounds, just note that. Any time we bring our attention to the present moment, we cultivate focus and stillness. And sometimes, silence.

Tune In to Your Thoughts
(BUT DON'T ALWAYS BELIEVE THEM!)

Thoughts can be intense and persuasive, but most of the time, they're not true—they're just stories and interpretations and misinterpretations. Our thoughts are with us constantly throughout the day, and often we're completely unaware of them and how much they influence our mood and behavior. Today, see if you can bring your awareness to your thoughts, just knowing *what* you are thinking *when* you are thinking it. And remember that you don't have to believe everything you think! You may notice that sometimes you have a thought such as "I'm not a good mother." With mindfulness, you can remind yourself that it's just a thought. You can say, "Right now, I'm just thinking I'm not a good mother." This subtle shift in how you approach your thoughts can make a dramatic change in your day.

BE *Effortless*

Simply sit in meditation and let your bones and gravity do most of the work of holding you in place. Allow your upper body to be upright, with your head resting gently on the spine. Roll your shoulders up and back to open up your chest, and release the tension in as many muscles as you can. The work your body does to hold you in various postures throughout the day doesn't account for a huge caloric burn, but it still takes energy. The gentle posture of meditation is soothing because it reduces the effort of your body.

Learn TO SINGLE-TASK

Everyone seems to pride themselves these days on multitasking, but the fact is, no one is actually good at it. The word "multitask" is a computer word, because computers can do all sorts of things, such as crunching numbers and sending emails and surfing the Internet, all at the same time. Humans cannot. So go easy on yourself, Mama. Do one thing at a time today. Make the lunches, *then* fold the laundry, *then* play blocks, *then* make the grocery list, *then* read some books. You'll get a lot more done, and feel a lot better about them, when you allow yourself to single-task.

MANTRA

I CAN STAY WITH THIS FEELING.

Feel THE GRAVITATIONAL PULL

Wherever you are right now, take a deep breath and feel the gentle pull of gravity, keeping you grounded and stable. Feel your body sinking into the chair or couch or bed, or feel your feet firmly on the earth. Notice the position of your body in relationship to the space around you. At any moment of the day, you can find stability by becoming aware of gravity.

KNOW YOUR *Default Setting*

We all have a set of default thoughts and behaviors that we tend to enact when we get frustrated or overwhelmed or angry—heavy sighing, loud yelling, quiet crying, self-critical thinking … With mindfulness, you can become more aware of these unthinking, knee-jerk reactions, and you can start to interrupt them with a moment of presence. Then you can respond with a wise choice, based on what's actually happening, instead of relying on ingrained habits that don't always serve you. Throughout your day, notice your default settings and reactions, and see if you can make these unconscious behaviors conscious.

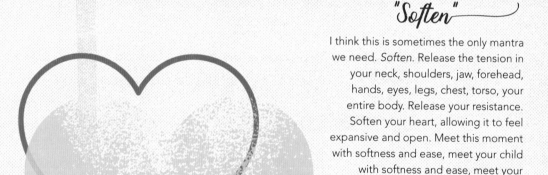

"*Soften*"

I think this is sometimes the only mantra we need. *Soften.* Release the tension in your neck, shoulders, jaw, forehead, hands, eyes, legs, chest, torso, your entire body. Release your resistance. Soften your heart, allowing it to feel expansive and open. Meet this moment with softness and ease, meet your child with softness and ease, meet your thoughts with softness and ease. Take a deep breath, and soften. Repeat the mantra "Soften."

BE OUT OF CONTROL

A big part of motherhood is making peace with things that are outside of your control, such as your toddler's ever-changing food preferences or your teen's early school start time. For this meditation, close your eyes and practice not controlling any part of your experience. Just allow your breath to be natural, without trying to breathe in any particular way. If thoughts arise, just let them be there, without stopping or engaging them. If you notice sensations in your body, see if you can allow them to be there, without scratching an itch or adjusting your posture or anything else you might be tempted to do to exert your will on your experience. Just practice being out of control.

FIND THE MOST *Important* THING

Perhaps one of the most enduring questions of the human experience is, "What is the most important thing I must do?" Russian novelist Leo Tolstoy had a great answer to that question over a century ago in his story "The Three Questions." When a king asked a wise man, "What is the most important thing I must do?", the wise man told him, "The thing you're doing *now*." Whatever you are doing right now, *that* is the most important thing. What would your days, and your life, be like if you did *every thing* as if it were the only, and the most important, thing to do?

MANTRA

I CAN
CALM
MYSELF
WITH
A DEEP
BREATH.

BE *Openly* AWARE

In many mindfulness exercises, we deliberately place our focus on a particular anchor, such as the breath (see, for example, page 20). However, with open awareness, we allow our attention to rest on whatever happens to be present. In this practice, you can close your eyes, begin breathing, and *just notice*—a thought, a cough, a twitch in your hand, a phone ringing, a memory, a softening in the jaw, the sound of a clock. It's not necessarily letting your mind wander, because you are paying attention, but you're also not constantly bringing your awareness back to your breath. Your only intention here is to be present to whatever arises. See if you can try this practice today, simply allowing your mind to rest on whatever captures your attention.

Know YOUR WHY

Why do you want to bring mindfulness and meditation into your life? There are lots of reasons to do it, but the most important one is YOURS. Why are you here, right now, reading these words? What do you need in your life? Peace, presence, comfort, connection, serenity, compassion, or all of the above? It can be hard to make changes to your habitual ways of acting, and it's even harder if you don't have a clear sense of purpose. Spend some time today reflecting on your why: *why do you want to practice mindfulness?* On the days when it's hard to find the time or energy to practice, your why will bring you back.

Breathe Out

When you breathe in, you activate the body's sympathetic nervous system (the "activating" and energizing part of the nervous system), and when you breathe out, you activate the parasympathetic nervous system, the so-called "relaxation response" of the body. One way to take advantage of the soothing effects of the out-breath is to lengthen your exhale deliberately; for example, you can breathe in for four counts, and then breathe out for six counts. When you need a moment of soothing today, take a deep breath in and really linger on the exhale.

"I Am Perfect
AS I AM"

Mindfulness is not about self-improvement. In fact, the fundamental insight of mindfulness is that you already have everything you need, right now in this moment. Right now you can breathe, you can find the clarity to see things as they are, and you can cultivate the wisdom to respond skillfully to what is in front of you. Mindfulness practice is not about changing who you are or trying to be a "better mother"; it's about learning to trust yourself as you find new ways to meet the challenges that arise each day. Repeat the mantra "I Am Perfect as I Am."

Notice YOUR RACE CAR MIND

It's totally okay when you notice you have not just a *racing* mind, but a *race car mind*: a mind that whips around the track at ridiculous speeds, and never seems to need refueling. Like that race car, your mind gets stuck on a track, revisiting the same terrain over and over again, instead of venturing somewhere new. When you notice your *race car mind*, see if you can get out of the driver's seat (because this vehicle will go on without you), and simply stand in the grass in the middle of the track. See if you can just watch the speeding car without being thrown about on hairpin turns, without your heart racing as fast as those wheels spin. See if you can be the observer of your thoughts, and not the driver.

Note HOW YOU PAY ATTENTION

One of my absolute favorite quotes about mindfulness comes from neuroscientist Sam Harris in his book *Waking Up*. He writes, "How we pay attention to the present moment largely determines the character of our experience and, therefore, the quality of our lives." Your day—and your life—is made up of an infinite number of present moments. How will you meet them? Notice the quality of the attention you bring to your present moments: Are you focused? Curious? Engaged? Impatient? How does the way you pay attention to those moments change your experience? How does the way you pay attention to your child change your interactions with her?

Ask, "HOW DO I KNOW?"

A helpful practice for cultivating a deeper awareness of your emotions is to ask yourself, "How do I *know* I am angry?" (or whatever you happen to be feeling.) Maybe you know you're angry because your jaw is clenched, or because the space between your eyes is pulsing, or because you have a strong desire to throw something. Whatever it is, ask yourself, "How do I know this is my experience?" This isn't about getting a "right" answer; it's simply a way to cultivate greater understanding.

Telescope YOUR ATTENTION

Sometimes we must attend to one small part of our experience (such as reading a book or playing a game), and other times we need to zoom out and take in a great deal of information at once (when we're driving, for example). You can play with this telescoping of attention in your mindfulness practice. First, bring your attention to your breath and your body, and stay with that for a few minutes. Then see if you can expand your attention to your surroundings, noticing the air, sounds, and smells around you. Finally, try to expand your attention even further, extending out of the room and into the outside world, noticing any sounds or sense impressions, or simply imagine your awareness is expanding outward and upward toward the sky. Then you can play with bringing your attention back to the room, and finally to your breath.

LABEL YOUR *Thoughts*

Noting is a powerful mindfulness practice for working with thoughts. When you notice a thought arise, either during your formal practice or as you're going about your day, see if you can acknowledge the thought with a simple label, such as "worrying," "judging," "remembering," or "planning." Don't worry about getting the label right—just "thinking" will do, too. In this way, you can notice the thought without getting entirely wrapped up in its contents. You can notice if the thought is loud or soft, pleasant or unpleasant, or short-lived or persistent. For today, practice labeling your thoughts, and then see what happens to them when you step back and don't get entangled in them.

Enjoy A MENTAL MASSAGE

Close your eyes, take a few deep breaths, and roll your shoulders back. Keeping your posture upright, allow yourself to release any tension in your neck and back. As you continue to focus on your breath, imagine someone gently placing her hands on the top of your head (you could even place your own hands there if you'd like). Imagine the feeling of warmth and soft pressure on your skull, and then pretend that her hands move to stroke your hair soothingly. Envision them lightly massaging your neck and shoulders, moving to exactly where you need relaxation. It might even help to think of a time you've had a pleasant massage or back rub, and remember the soothing sensations. Take a deep breath and savor this feeling of being nurtured and cared for.

TAKE A *Pause*

We often bring our attention to the breath in mindfulness because it is always with us, and directing our attention to the bodily experience of breathing gets us out of our heads and creates some distance from our thoughts. One way to practice mindful breathing is with an ever-so-slight pause between the in-breath and the out-breath, and between the out-breath and the in-breath. Notice the sensations of this liminal moment. Practice attending to the distinct sensations of the in-breath compared to those of the out-breath. Can you experience breathing in and breathing out as two separate events?

Don't Wait FOR THE WORLD TO GET QUIET AROUND YOU

I once taught mindfulness to elementary students in a very noisy and chaotic after-school program. Sometimes the kids would get frustrated when we were trying to practice our mindfulness and everyone else was being loud and distracting. I told them, "If we wait for the world to get quiet around us, we're going to be waiting for a very long time." Mindfulness isn't something we practice only when the conditions are perfect—it's something that helps us create peace and quiet in ourselves as we move through a noisy and chaotic world.

MANTRA

I CAN NOTICE WHAT'S HAPPENING RIGHT NOW.

HANDLE YOUR Feelings

As if emotions weren't complicated enough, we also have feelings about our feelings! We tell ourselves that we "shouldn't" be upset with our child or resentful of our partner, or that certain emotions, such as anger or frustration, are not acceptable. When you notice this happening, remind yourself that all emotional experiences are simply a part of the human condition, and that whatever you are feeling is okay. Anything that can be experienced can also be worked with, so take a deep breath and investigate your emotion, your needs, and what you could do to take care of yourself.

Listen
TO YOUR BODY

Your emotions are almost always physical before they are conscious— there's a pit in your stomach, a trembling in your hands, or a new tension in your jaw that alerts you that something important is happening. Today, practice being aware of your body and the signals it sends. See if you can identify the unique markers of different emotions in your system, such as when you feel sad, angry, jealous, or happy. Cultivating this deep attunement with your body and its messages is a core component of emotional awareness.

JUST *Note* GONE

Mindfulness teacher Shinzen Young describes a slightly more advanced mindfulness practice he calls "just note gone." It's an "advanced" practice because it's somewhat easy to notice what is here, and present, but much more difficult to notice what is NOT here. We often don't recognize when the headache goes away, or when the thought ends. For today, practice noting "gone." If you were aware of something, and then you eventually realize it's not there anymore, "just note gone." Don't worry about getting it at the instant it disappears; just acknowledge that what was once present has now shifted.

MANTRA

I AM

NOT MY

THOUGHTS.

Check
YOUR POSTURE

There is an amazing relationship between how we hold our body, and how we feel. If we stand upright, with our shoulders back and our feet grounded on the earth, we feel confident and powerful. Try experimenting right now with standing up tall and proud, and notice how that feels. Then allow yourself to slouch, let your head droop forward, and draw your feet together as your body folds in on itself. Do you notice a difference? For today, practice checking in with your posture. Are you in a position that conveys alertness and confidence? Can you make subtle shifts in your body and see how that feels?

Try NOT TO Follow THE THOUGHT

It's easy when a thought comes up in meditation to think, "This is *really* important—I need to address this thought before it goes away." Thoughts are seductive, and are great at convincing us that we must act upon them immediately. See if you can resist the temptation to interrupt your practice to chase a thought, jot down more to-dos, or solve a problem. Trust that the stillness and receptivity you cultivate in your mindfulness practice will allow a deeper knowing to emerge once you allow all the surface chatter in your mind to settle. Stay on your cushion and stay with your practice.

MANTRA

I AM

FOCUSED

ON THIS

TASK.

I CAN DO

JUST THIS.

MINDFUL MOMENT
Meditation

Breathe in and notice any tension in the body.
Breathe out and release the tension.
Breathe in and notice if judgments or
thoughts are present.
Breathe out and remember that
thoughts are just thoughts.
Breathe in and notice any emotions
that are present.
Breathe out and know that
this emotion is not you.
Breathe in and smile.
Breathe out and relax.

Practice COHERENT BREATHING

Some amazing scientists studied the "most relaxing" rate of breathing, and discovered that it's about five or six breaths per minute (compared to the average adult breathing rate of 12–15 breaths per minute). To practice coherent breathing, you can use a timer, or you can simply count in your head as you breathe in and out. To breathe six times per minute, count to five on the inhale, using all 5 seconds for your breath. It's important to make the in-breath last for the full 5 seconds, as opposed to taking a quick breath in and holding it. Then count to five on the exhale, slowly releasing the breath. Try it for 2 minutes and see how it feels. Do you feel more relaxed?

Note AVOIDANCE

It's natural for our mindfulness practice to ebb and flow, to have times when we're committed to our daily meditation habit, and times when we just can't find our way to the cushion. But if you notice a pattern of avoiding your mindfulness or meditation time, do some gentle inquiry to figure out why. Dodging your practice can be the focus of your practice! What stories are you telling yourself about why you're not making time for mindfulness? Are difficult thoughts or emotions arising when you meditate? Bring some curiosity and compassion to your avoidance, remind yourself why you started this practice in the first place, and see if you can identify what's standing in your way.

CREATE *Spaciousness*

Feeling *spacious* is the opposite of feeling tense, closed-off, and contracted. Take a few deep breaths and see if you can bring some spaciousness and expansion to your body—open up your chest, spread out your fingers and toes, stretch your arms above your head, and open your jaw. Take a few deep breaths and imagine each breath is an invitation to greater openness, relaxation, acceptance, and tranquility.

CHAPTER 2

Starting the Day

MORNING PRACTICES

Mornings offer a bewildering array of experiences. One morning you may be able to linger in the sweetness and stillness of the first few moments of a day when the world has not yet demanded much of you. And then on other days the morning is a chaotic blur of being woken early (after a night full of interruptions), dragging older kids out of bed, getting breakfasts and backpacks ready, ushering everyone out the door, and getting yourself to work on time.

Mornings can be a great time to practice mindfulness, however, because no matter what the day has in store for you, you can begin with a few moments of mindful reflection that prepare you to meet the new day with intention and presence.

THE
First Moment
OF YOUR DAY

If you can, don't rush yourself out of bed in the morning. A fussing child can wait for 30 seconds while you gently stretch. Feel the movement of your body, and consider your intention for the day (see page 42). If you have a few more seconds, take a deep breath in, welcoming the strength and energy you will need for your day, and then breathe out while you imagine releasing worries and tension and anything else you don't need today.

EMBODIED
Presence

As you wake in the morning, can you become aware of the process of shifting from sleep to wakefulness? When you rouse from sleep, there is a brief experience of spaciousness, as consciousness is still a bit fuzzy in the movement from your dream state to awakening. Can you feel yourself "move back in" to your body? Can you sense this re-embodying that happens each morning? Set an intention today to be mindful of your body, bringing careful attention to movements and sensations as you move through your day. See if you can live fully in your body today.

Early Morning MEDITATION

If you can, wake up 10 minutes (or more, if you'd like) earlier than your children. Sit upright on a cushion or your couch or your bed, and set a timer for 10 minutes. Close your eyes and bring your attention to your breath, and notice what it feels like to be awake when everyone else is sleeping. What sounds do you hear? Does the house feel different? Do you feel different? Morning meditations can sometimes be "easier" because the day has yet to intrude on your experience, and your busy, chattering mind may still be a bit sleepy. Experiment with early morning practice and what it feels like for you.

SET YOUR *Intention*

As you begin your day, set an intention. Your intention is not your to-do list, it's your guidance for how you want to be in the world today. How do you want to feel? How do you want your child to feel? How do you want to show up today? Some of the mantras in this chapter might be your intentions for the day, and are meant for when you want to focus on just one aspect of mindfulness practice for a day.

MANTRA

I WELCOME TODAY.

WHAT'S YOUR *Morning Story?*

We're always telling stories, and you probably have a story about mornings. You might tell yourself that mornings are chaotic and stressful, that the kids will wake up cranky and hate the breakfast you make, that everyone will feel rushed, and you'll still end up leaving the house late. While you certainly don't know how any one morning will actually turn out, see if you can approach your morning routine with a blank slate. Assuming the morning will be a disaster can sometimes make it so, as we end up filtering everything through our dim-colored glasses. Try welcoming the morning as a new experience, and even if things don't go the way you planned, you'll at least feel a lot calmer as it happens.

"TODAY I WILL PRACTICE *Enthusiasm*"

Today I will bring eagerness. I will approach everything I do as if it were the most important thing to be doing (for in many ways, it is). I will bring energy and excitement and enthusiasm to my day, and I will notice how it feels to see each moment as worthy of intense interest and commitment.

"TODAY I WILL PRACTICE *Appreciation*"

Today I will notice all that I can be thankful for. I will appreciate even the littlest of joys, and I will be grateful for the opportunities to learn from difficult moments. I will express my gratitude for others, and honor the qualities I appreciate in myself.

"TODAY I WILL PRACTICE *Authenticity*"

Today I will be myself. Today I will give voice to my needs and my feelings, even if it's only to myself. I will not try to hide or cover up; I will be authentically me.

MORNING *Body Scan*

In whatever posture is comfortable (lying down, sitting in a chair, nursing your baby on the couch), take a deep breath and bring your attention to your lower body (legs and feet). Just notice the sensations that are present, if any, and take a moment to set an intention for how you want to move in the world today—do you want to slow down, or will you need to be a bit speedier and more efficient today? Bring your awareness to your torso, noticing the sensations in your chest and belly. With your next breath, set an intention for how you want to feel today—energetic, restful, joyful, peaceful, or something else? Then gently bring your attention to your arms and hands, and set an intention for how you will be with your children today, imagining them in your embrace. Finally, bring your awareness to your neck and face and head, and set an intention for how you will be present today. Take a few more deep breaths, and begin your day.

"TODAY I WILL PRACTICE *Play*"

Today I will allow myself to have fun. I will play with my kids and not worry about whether I'm being productive. I will seek joy and cultivate play.

"TODAY I WILL PRACTICE *Empathy*"

Today I will do my best to see the world from other perspectives. I will bring compassion and understanding to my child's suffering, no matter how trivial it may seem. I will seek understanding and practice empathy.

"TODAY I WILL PRACTICE *Understanding*"

Today I will listen with the intent to understand. I won't get caught up in thinking about what I'm going to say or do, or how I'm going to fix a problem. I will listen to others and seek to know and comprehend their experience.

"TODAY I WILL PRACTICE *Self-Compassion*"

Today I will speak kindly to myself. When things are difficult, I will take care of my needs without guilt. I will remember that the things that are hard for me are hard for everyone. I will offer love to myself without reservation or qualification.

"TODAY I WILL PRACTICE *Acceptance*"

Today I will accept. I will allow my thoughts, my feelings, and my experiences to be as they are. I will know that I am *enough*, just as I am right now.

WHAT IS THE STATE OF *My Nervous System?*

Before you move into your day, check in with your nervous system. Do you feel calm and stable? Or is your heart racing and your breath shallow? We are social animals, and the state of our nervous system impacts the nervous systems of those around us, including our children. If you feel agitated, take a few deep breaths, focusing on really allowing the belly to expand on the inhale, and then engaging the diaphragm on the exhale as you squeeze the air out of your lungs (you'll feel a sensation like you're trying to bring your belly button to your spine). Continue with a few deep breaths until you can feel your system begin to stabilize. This will allow you to share your calm, peaceful state with your children as they begin their day.

"TODAY I WILL PRACTICE *Creativity*"

Today I will seek out opportunities to create—I will color or paint or dance or sing or write or sew. I will practice discovery and innovation.

Morning Coffee MEDITATION

Make some time today to truly savor the first few sips of your morning coffee or tea, instead of pouring a hot cup and then letting it get cold as you attend to more pressing concerns. Allow yourself a few moments to feel the warmth of the beverage where your hands make contact with the cup. Take a deep breath and inhale the rich aroma. Drink slowly and really taste the flavor of your morning libation. Notice the sensations in your throat and belly as you swallow. Perhaps even spend a silent moment in gratitude for caffeine and all it will help you do today.

"TODAY I WILL PRACTICE *Movement*"

Today I will move with intention and awareness. I will be fully in my body, noticing my internal sensations as well as my body's interactions with the world. I will move in ways that feel good and nurturing and healthy for my body.

HOLD YOUR *Intentions* LIGHTLY

You probably have a lot of things you want to get done today, and ways that you want to be today. Honor those intentions for your day, but hold them lightly. The world is not aware of your agenda, and your day may have other plans for you. Celebrate the things you accomplish, and greet the wrinkles and curveballs and unexpected roadblocks with as much patience and presence and compassion as you can. You may have set the intention to tackle a long to-do list today, but instead you had to pick up your sick child from school. Allow your intention to shift as the events of your day unfold. Intentions should create a general direction and tone for your day, not dictate the precise path you must follow.

"TODAY I WILL PRACTICE *Contentment*"

Today I will not strive. Today I will not get caught in wanting. Today I will practice being okay with what I have, who I am, and who my children are. Today I will be content.

Morning MANTRA

Today I will be present.
Today I will pause before
responding.
Today I will hold my children
and myself with compassion.
Today I will welcome my
experiences, and try to
meet each moment
without resistance.
Today I will do my best, and
be kind to myself when I know
I could have done better.
Today I will be present.

"I'LL *Handle* WHAT TODAY BRINGS"

When we get upset because things don't go according to our plan, it's often because we weren't aware of our plan in the first place, and we didn't recognize that we had an assumption that things would go our way. Notice what you're expecting today, so you can skillfully meet the moments that don't deliver. Repeat the mantra: "I'll Handle What Today Brings."

MANTRA

TODAY I WILL

BE PRESENT.

"TODAY I WILL PRACTICE *Quiet*"

Today I will welcome quiet and stillness. I will not try to fill silences that do not need filling, and I will make time for moments of peace and calm.

Breakfast MEDITATION

If you tend to skip breakfast, see if you can take a few moments to eat something healthy this morning, perhaps some yogurt or a piece of fruit, or peanut butter and banana on toast. If you can, try to really taste and enjoy the food, instead of eating on-the-go. Even if you only get three bites in silence, savor each one and allow eating breakfast to be a truly nourishing, if brief, experience.

MORNING *Yoga*

Cats and dogs always stretch when they first get up, and we probably should, too. You can do some simple yoga as part of your morning practice—stand with your feet hip distance apart and stretch your arms up above your head (a lovely posture to welcome a new day). Get down on your hands and knees and gently round your back upward as you tuck your chin to your chest, and then drop your belly toward the floor as you lift your chin and your chest. This is more about moving and stretching your body in a way that feels good and nurturing than it is about getting a posture right. Listen to what your body needs.

"TODAY I WILL PRACTICE *Rest*"

Today I will rest. I will allow myself to nap, and I will claim renewal when I need it.

"TODAY I WILL PRACTICE *Wonder*"

Today I will welcome delight and surprise. I'll do my best to bring my attention to the little things I often overlook. I'll approach my day with a sense of enchantment and fascination and wonder.

Morning Walk

If it's an option for you, walk with your child to school this morning and leave a few minutes early. Take your time to be mindful of your surroundings—pay attention to the sights and sounds of the morning, such as the sun rising, birds singing, and traffic buzzing. Share your hopes and plans for the day with your child and enjoy a pleasant morning walk.

MANTRA

TODAY IS
A CHANCE
TO START
AGAIN.

MANTRA

TODAY IS

THE MOST

IMPORTANT

DAY.

DOES *Today's* TO-DO LIST *Include You*?

You may start your morning by running through your to-do list … and you may discover *you* are not on it at all. You've got the kids' homework and music lessons, the packages that need to be dropped off, and the projects that must be completed for work … but where are *you*? Like many mothers, you may get to the end of the day and have forgotten to take care of yourself. Take a moment to be mindful of your needs today (do you need to book a haircut? can you make it to yoga class?) and see if you can put yourself on the to-do list.

"TODAY I WILL PRACTICE *Trust*"

Today I will trust that I know just what I need, and just what my child needs. I will trust that I have, within me, all the wisdom and peace and stillness and love that I need.

EMBRACE *Today*

Today will unfold in its own special way. It's not predetermined, but it's also not fully up to you. Show up with presence, pause before acting, and engage with today the best way you know how.

Morning COMMUTE

If your morning routine involves driving the children to daycare or school, those moments in the car can sometimes be the most stressful of your day—kids, even just one, fussing in the backseat while you try to focus on driving and mentally prepare for the day ahead. It can help to remind yourself that the commute is a short part of your day, and by the time you get home, the stressors of the morning are often long forgotten. Take a deep breath and focus on *this moment*, instead of letting your thoughts drift to "This *always* happens!" or "Tomorrow will be *exactly* like this, too." If you notice the same conflicts each morning, see if you can make some changes, such as putting snacks within your child's reach in the backseat or downloading some kid-friendly tunes to listen to during your drive.

CHAPTER 3

Nurture

MINDFUL MOTHERHOOD

If being a mindful mother doesn't mean we're perfect, what does it mean? Well, it simply means we apply the practice of mindfulness to motherhood. It means we cultivate presence, awareness, and non-judgment, we nurture and resource ourselves, and we do our best to approach our emotions and stress mindfully, so we can parent with empathy, attentiveness, peacefulness, and ease. The following meditations and mantras will help you in this challenging endeavor.

Meditation INTERRUPTUS

As a mother, the chances that your quiet meditation session will be interrupted are approximately 100 percent. But when your peaceful silence is broken by a young person needing your attention, the meditation doesn't need to end. You can simply shift your awareness from your breath to your child. *Mindfulness is about paying attention to whatever is happening right now.* During formal practice, breathing is happening, and when your child arrives parenting is happening. You can bring your kind and careful attention to this moment with your child.

MANTRA

I AM

DOING

THE BEST

I CAN.

DON'T "FIND" TIME. *Make Time*

As mothers, we often put "time for myself" pretty low on our list of priorities. It becomes something to do "when I find the time." But the problem is *we never find the time!* If we want time to ourselves—to pause and breathe, to take a hot shower, or to savor a cup of coffee—we need to *make* the time. Pay attention to how you use your time today. Do you notice that there are periods of "wasted" time that could be used for nourishing self-care? Are there commitments that you can drop from your routine? See if you can make time in your day that's just for you!

KEEP YOUR *Sense of Humor*

You know the phrase, "Some day you'll look back on all this and laugh"? Given what we know about our ability to sustain attention and remember things, we probably won't get around to laughing at it "some day," so why not today? Can you be so present with what's happening that you see not only the difficult, but the hilarious? Yes, it's annoying when you need to leave the house and your five-year-old is running around in his underwear humming the "Star Wars" theme while pretending to wield a light saber, but that's also really funny. So go ahead and laugh.

Nurture YOUR BODY

Your ability to handle stressors and summon the energy to do all that you need to do today depends on how you treat your body—what you eat, how you move, and when you sleep. Be mindful of what you eat, seeing if you can opt for something healthy (bonus points if it has protein), instead of mindlessly snacking on sugary foods that don't fuel your body. Find opportunities to move your body, even it's not "exercise"— walk to the store, or park at the far end of the parking lot. Take the stairs instead of the elevator, go for a short walk at lunch, or use the 10 minutes before the kids get home from school for a quick cardio workout.

"I AM *Perfectly* IMPERFECT"

There's so much pressure to be a SuperMama, but no mother is perfect. Being mindful doesn't mean we will do everything right, but it will certainly help us stay connected to our intentions. We will bring our loving attention and presence to the important work of mothering. We will notice when we are not acting in a way that aligns with our deepest values, and then we'll hold ourselves with compassion as we begin again. We will notice, too, the moments that feel amazing and delightful, the times when we *do* feel like a SuperMama, and appreciate our gifts and actions that made those moments possible. Repeat the mantra "I Am Perfectly Imperfect," and remember that this is exactly what your children need you to be.

Nurture YOUR *Relationship*

Sometimes our relationship with our partner looks like one between crabby roommates instead of a committed couple. See if you can make some time today that's just for the two of you, even if it's only 10 minutes after the children are in bed. Share the celebrations and frustrations of your day, and communicate any needs you may have. Pay attention to how you speak to your partner—do you start in with complaints or the negative parts of your day? When you need something from your partner, do you present it as a demand or a request? Can you mindfully listen to each other and find solutions that meet both of your needs?

"IT'S *Okay*"

It's okay to have a day when …
- The beds don't get made, but art projects do
- Soccer practice gets skipped, but long naps don't
- Popcorn is served for dinner, and ice cream for dessert
- The to-do list remains long, because our time with our children is short.

On these days, remember to tell yourself, "It's okay."

HOW DO YOU *Speak* TO YOURSELF?

Do you speak to yourself in ways you would never permit another person to speak to you? Your self-talk matters: negative self-talk can trigger your stress response, and it just makes you feel miserable. For today, pay attention to your inner voice. Are you speaking to yourself as you would a dear friend, or your own child? Are you treating yourself with understanding and compassion? If you notice that you're being overly critical, see if you can offer yourself some kindness instead.

"I AM AT *Peace* IN THE STORM"

Mindful motherhood is about *being in the center*, about finding the space of calm weather in the eye of the storm. I don't mean you need to find some woo-woo "heart center." I mean you should *literally find your center.* While the tantrums and mealtimes and arguments and snuggles and messes and kisses swirl around us, we find stability in the center as we embrace the totality of motherhood. You can find this by practicing the introductory exercises in Chapter 1, and through engaging in self-care practices that nourish your soul and allow you to feel stabilized in the midst of chaos and change. Repeat the mantra "I Am at Peace in the Storm."

MANTRA

I DESERVE CARE AND EMPATHY.

"*Thanks*,
BUT I'VE GOT THIS"

This is my favorite mantra for when my inner critic likes to offer up words such as, "You're a terrible mother" or "You are never going to be any good at this." I simply say "Thanks for the input. I know you're just doing the whole *worrying* thing that your part of my brain is supposed to be doing. But I've GOT this."

PHONE *Awareness*

Most of us spend too much time on our phones; they are designed to capture our attention, and leave us craving more stimulation. You can bring your mindful awareness to your phone habits by putting a special picture on your lock screen that reminds you to ask yourself, "What am I looking for? What do I need?" when you pick up your phone. If you're looking for directions to a playdate, then your phone is the perfect place to go. If you're looking for connection, or if you're bored or lonely, then maybe the phone isn't really what you need right now. You don't need to ditch your phone all together, but you can be more mindful of what you're using it for.

When you put down your phone, *notice how you feel*. Did you just laugh at a goofy cat video and now you feel relaxed and happy? Great! Did you just check Instagram and now you feel completely miserable and totally inferior after seeing the perfect-looking meals and art projects and home repairs all the other mothers are doing? Hmmm … This isn't about judging yourself for being on your phone, but simply taking in the information your body is giving you about how the way you spend your time impacts how you feel.

Nurture YOUR MIND

We must be mindful not only of the foods we consume, but the information and media that we consume, too. If the news is too overwhelming and negative, spend some time with a good book instead. If your typical TV fare is "mindless," mix it up with a top-rated documentary. It's great to have our "guilty pleasures," but it's also important to nourish our minds.

Ambivalence is Okay

It is completely normal and absolutely okay to have mixed feelings about motherhood. It seems that publicly, we're only allowed to talk about the joys of parenting, or, if we do talk about the hard parts, we have to make a joke about it that in some way delegitimizes our frustrations. Some days you will love being a mother, and some days you may dread it. Some days you'll laugh and wonder how you ever lived without these little darlings in your life, and some days you may ask yourself why you ever became a mother. As psychologist Harriet Lerner writes in *The Mother Dance*, "Raising children, for both men and women, is neither intrinsically wonderful nor intrinsically terrible. It is almost always both." With mindfulness, you can make peace with the "both-and" of motherhood: it is *both* incredibly hard *and* incredibly wonderful. And that's okay.

DITCH THE SCRIPT AND *Embrace* IMPROV

It would be lovely if our mama-day went entirely by the script, with perfectly behaved children who make skillful choices and utter kind words all day long. But our children are not actors in our screenplay, they are our partners in an improv sketch. Instead of a carefully choreographed production, we jam together in a dynamic freestyle. In improvisation mode, we pay attention to the energy and action of our partner, and respond in kind. When the scene changes or the song ends, we have no choice but to go with it. There's a lot more uncertainty with improv, but the performance is usually pretty amazing. So when your two-year-old decides that dumping the blocks all over the living room (over and over again!) is more fun than building the castle you had suggested, see if you can join him in his wild world, rather than forcing him into yours.

MANTRA

I DON'T NEED TO BE PERFECT.

EVERYDAY *Self-Care*

We must nurture ourselves if we are going to nurture our children each day. This means self-care should be as important a part of our day as brushing our teeth and eating healthy food. Self-care isn't just adding in a few side dishes of massages and pedicures—it's an essential ingredient that must be baked into our days. Find the things you can do every day that nourish you—a brief walk outside, a warm cup of tea, a good book before bed, a nap when your little one naps, a few minutes of meditation—and make them an integral part of your daily routine.

MANTRA

WHAT DO I NEED?

Playing VS WINNING

Research shows that athletes perform better when they focus on playing to *play*, instead of playing to *win*. Instead of trying to get a #motherhoodwin, see if you can just focus on the act of being a mother. Parent in *this* moment, responding to the needs of *this* moment, without trying to *win* the moment. That doesn't mean you can't have intentions for how you will be and how your children will be, but if you focus too intently on winning and arriving at a set destination, you'll miss the journey of getting there, and perhaps a few fun side trips along the way.

Take Care OF YOU FOR YOU

A common justification (as if one was needed) for mothers to take care of themselves is that they need to do it for their children: if a *mother* isn't nurtured, how can she nurture others? There's nothing wrong with this argument—it's undoubtedly true. But you can also take care of yourself just because you are a human being worthy of self-love and care. You can certainly take care of yourself because it's good for your kids, but it can also be *just about you.*

Empathy DOES NOT MEAN AGREEMENT

You can empathize with your child without agreeing with her or letting her emotions run the show. You can let your child know you understand that it's hard to get ready for bed when she's been having fun playing, but still ensure that she gets to bed on time. Don't hold back on empathy because you think it means indulging her whims or agreeing that you are being "mean." Empathy is an important way of validating her experience.

A *Balanced* APPROACH TO BALANCE

We often talk about wanting to "find balance," as if it were a solid thing we must discover or a destination where we must arrive. But it's much more helpful to think of balance as a dance. In fact, in ballet, a *balance* is a move performed by gently shifting your weight from one foot to the other, and I think that's a healthier way to approach balance. Sometimes you lean into your work, sometimes you lean harder into family time, but you're rarely completely still, holding everything up all at once in some complicated pose. Balance is not something we achieve; it's something we do. It's a dance.

A *Loving Kindness* MEDITATION FOR YOU

Take a deep breath and place your hand on your heart. Imagine sending yourself as much love and acceptance as you can, and silently repeat the following phrases to yourself:

May I be happy.
May I be healthy.
May I be safe.
May I be peaceful.
May I be present.
May I be accepting.
May I be kind to myself.
May I be patient.
May I be curious.
May I be engaged.
May I be hopeful.
May I be loved.
May I be loving.
May I be joyful.
May I be full of life.

Peace AND *Stillness* ARE ALWAYS AVAILABLE

No matter what is happening in your day, peace and stillness are always only a breath (or five!) away. You'd be amazed at how soothing just 10 seconds of being fully aware of your breathing can be. If you notice yourself becoming agitated, remind yourself that *peace can always be found within you.* You have everything you need. Always.

Change IS THE ONLY CONSTANT

With mindfulness, we embrace change, because it is one of the few
things that we know for certain will happen. Just when you get into
a groove, or when you think you've figured everything out, things will
change again. It's a completely natural and necessary process as you and
your children grow and move through the world together. See if you can
welcome change as your partner in this unpredictable adventure.

MANTRA

HOW CAN I TAKE CARE OF MYSELF RIGHT NOW?

"I CAN'T DO IT ALL AT ONCE"

I'll be honest, I've rebelled against this mantra
many times, but each time I do, I realize its
frustrating truth: we simply cannot do it all,
all at the same time. If I divide my limited
energy among *all the things* I want to do,
I end up with a complicated equation that
will never balance. I've learned there are
times when I need to put one of my passions
on hold, times when I have to lean in and do
something difficult, and times when space
opens up that's just for me. I've learned it's
more about bringing my all to all that I do,
and trusting that I *can* do it all, just not all at
once. So when you're juggling too many
things, gently remind yourself, "I Can't Do
It All at Once."

Celebrate
SMALL VICTORIES

Did everyone get dressed today? Did everyone eat their veggies today? Did you have only a small outburst instead of a big one? Did you have a whole meal where no one argued? Yay! It's important not to overlook the small victories you have each day. Take a moment to be mindful of and honor all the little things that went right today.

NURTURE YOUR
Friendships

While Facebook and text messages offer great ways to stay in digital touch with our friends, there's no substitute for old-fashioned analog communication. Instead of texting back and forth, can you give your friend a call and chat for a few minutes? Could you even find some time to meet for coffee?

WE'RE NOT MEANT
TO DO THIS ALONE

As mothers, we're sometimes isolated, and we may think we're the only one having a tough time. We may not be able to see that other mothers have similar struggles, or feel that we can lean on them for support. It's incredibly clichéd, but it does take a village to do the work of motherhood. We were never meant to mother alone in the suburbs. Do what you can to reach out to other mothers, either through a mothers group, your local community center, or even in online forums and Facebook groups. It's important to find your village.

Motherhood STORIES

We all have stories in our mind about what motherhood should be like and how mothers should act, and those stories influence how we feel about ourselves. It's helpful to spend some time considering the things you tell yourself or believe about motherhood, such as "Motherhood should come naturally," or "Good mothers never yell at their children." Sometimes these stories operate under the surface, and cause us a lot of pain when we don't live up to our unstated expectations. The truth is, motherhood will be what it is for *you*, and the more aware you are of your stories, the less you will add to your own suffering by thinking you are somehow "doing it wrong."

YOU DON'T HAVE TO *Engage* YOUR CHILD ALL THE TIME

Just like you, your child needs quiet time and down time. Even an infant needs wakeful time without stimulation or engagement so that he can curiously and quietly observe his world. Putting pressure on yourself to always entertain and engage your child will exhaust *both* of you. Ensuring that everyone has down time and some brief alone time during the day will make your playtime that much richer and more enjoyable.

A MINDFUL *Shower*

Going to the spa is out of the question most days, but can you be completely present when you shower or take a bath? Enjoy the sensation of warm water on your skin, savor the scent of a favorite body wash, pay attention to the soothing sounds of running water. Instead of letting your mind wander to your to-do list, or running through your day in your head, just let your shower be a time to wash, and to care for yourself.

Noticing GUILT

Guilt is probably a universal component of motherhood. We can be incredibly hard on ourselves when we focus on our shortcomings and mistakes. When you experience guilt, take a moment to notice the feeling and what is triggering it. Is there something to learn from it? Is it a signal that in some way you're not honoring your intentions or values? If so, thank your guilt for providing you with this helpful information, and see what changes you may need to make. See if you can forgive yourself (see page 108), remind yourself that no one is perfect, and honor yourself for doing the best you can.

OWN YOUR *Emotion*

It's tempting to think that we're upset because the *kids* made a mess, or because our *partner* came home late, or the *dog* won't be quiet. *But our emotions are always about us and our own needs.* If the kids make a mess, our anger isn't because of *their* actions, it's because of *our* need for order, or cleanliness, or something else that a mess-free house gives us. For today, bring some curiosity to the emotions you experience, and see if you can identify the underlying need beneath your feelings. This practice allows you to gain some ownership over your experience, and empowers you to consider how you can best meet your needs.

You can take ownership over your emotions further by investigating whether you are blaming someone else for your sensitivity. Sometimes we inadvertently let our children think that they *caused* our feelings ("I wouldn't be so upset if you hadn't hit your brother …"). That places a big burden on a little set of shoulders; our children shouldn't have to feel responsible for our emotions. If you share your feelings with your child, you can say, "I'm upset right now because it's important to me that we all feel safe in our home." This shift in describing your emotional experience removes any defensiveness your child might feel, and opens the way for a conversation about how everyone can help create a safe and loving home.

THIS AGE IS THE BEST!

A friend of mine once told me that she would frequently tell herself, "This age is the *best.* She's so *fun* right now!" And then a few months later, she'd remark, "No, *this* age is the best! Look at what she's doing *now!*" For all their challenges, each stage of childhood has its bests. Just imagine what it would be like to raise your children always knowing that the stage they're in right now is truly the best.

TWO-MINUTE *Self-Care*

Self-care doesn't have to be extensive or expensive. There are lots of things you can do in just two minutes (or less) that can nourish you and give you some refueling during your day. If you have just two minutes, you can:

- Drink a full glass of water
- Step outside and take some deep breaths
- Close your eyes and breathe
- Call or text a friend
- Listen to your favorite song
- Do a few gentle yoga stretches or poses.

Knowing YOUR TRIGGERS

There are lots of things that can upset us during the day, and it's helpful to know exactly what those things are, because we're often wrong about them. For the next week, keep a "Trigger Tracker" where you write down the specific incidents or behaviors that cause you to "lose it." You might start to notice a pattern: it's always at a particular time of day, or it's because of a particular request, or something else. You may realize that the actual trigger is not what you thought it was (for example, sometimes in my work with mothers, they discover that, with all apologies to the guys out there, it's actually their husbands triggering them, and not their kids!) Take some time to investigate your triggers and see what you notice.

Time of Day	Trigger/ Event	Reaction	What I Noticed

WHEN *Self-Care* ISN'T SKILLFUL

Sometimes mothers tell me that their self-care strategies aren't very skillful—they know they *should* go for a walk or drink some water or take a nap or meditate, but instead they waste time on social media or binge-watch TV or buy things they don't need. Those activities aren't necessarily "bad," but if you're not feeling nurtured, it may be because the strategies you use aren't really meeting your needs. If you notice this pattern, take some time to see what you're trying to find when you engage in these not-as-helpful self-care practices. Are you looking for connection? Support? Novelty? Once you know what needs you are trying to fulfill, you can look for other ways to meet them, such as calling a friend or joining a book group.

Leave WORK AT WORK

It's hard to arrive home and be fully with your family if your head is still at work. Perhaps it might help to do a "mind dump" before you leave work, writing down all that you need to focus on tomorrow and the things that you don't want to forget. Take a few deep breaths as you think about leaving the work part of your day behind, and transitioning home. Then when you get home, you can be completely present with your children.

WHEN *Me-Time* IS OVER

It can be hard to shift back into mothering mode after you've been in "me-time" mode. Mothers tell me that they don't want the bliss of self-care and rest to come to an end, and find themselves dreading the end of their alone time. It's a completely natural response to try to cling to the tranquility of quiet moments to yourself, but it's really the *clinging* that makes it painful, not the ending. This is the basis of much of our suffering, when we crave pleasant experiences and then try to hold on to them tightly when we find them. See if you can practice being so fully present with "me-time" that there's no grasping—there's just peaceful time to yourself. If you can fully experience and inhabit your moments of self-care, it will be easier to transition out of those moments and into the next ones.

CHAPTER 4

Sustain

MINDFULNESS THROUGHOUT THE DAY

Mindfulness is both a formal practice, and something
we cultivate throughout the day. Mindfulness teacher
Jon Kabat-Zinn likes to ask, "When does the meditation end?"
Just because we've gotten up from our cushion doesn't mean we
fall back into our regular mode of distraction and over-reaction.
Use the practices in this chapter to sustain your mindfulness
practice over the course of your day.

DRIVING *Meditation*

You would think we'd always be paying attention while driving, but in fact we are usually on auto-pilot. Today, try to be more mindful when you drive. Pay close attention not just to the road in front of you, but notice all that your body does as you drive—the pressure of your foot on the gas, the movement of your hands on the steering wheel. When you hit a red light, just sit at the red light. Notice if there's any restlessness. Turn off the radio and just notice what it's like to drive through your part of the world, truly aware of the things you often just, well, drive by.

DROP *In*

At any moment of your day, you can "drop in": drop in to your body and notice what you are feeling. Notice your feet on the floor. Notice where you are and what you are doing. Just drop in to presence.

Nap-Time MEDITATION

If your children still take naps, use nap time as a moment of quiet reflection for yourself. Close your eyes and take a few (or many!) deep breaths. What has gone well so far today? What can you honor yourself for doing? Take a moment to soak in the good that has already happened. Consider what has been difficult today, and what you can do in the remaining hours to take care of yourself as you care for your child.

THE *Best Time of Day* FOR MEDITATION

The best time of day for meditation is the time of day when *you* will meditate—i.e. it is different for everyone. I prefer early morning, because the house is quiet, and I like knowing that the first thing I do in the day is just for me. But you need to find the time that will work for you. When are you most alert and least likely to get interrupted? It's helpful to pick a time that's relatively consistent, as this will help you keep your habit going. If morning doesn't work for you, see if you can practice during your lunchtime, during nap time, or before bed.

Simplify

See if you can do one thing each day to simplify your life. Organize a drawer in the kitchen, cancel an appointment that's not necessary, or finally get all those apps on your phone into folders. If your children are old enough, you can invite them to help—they can organize one drawer in their bedroom, throw out dried-up markers and glue sticks, or fill a bag with books to donate. It's amazing how creating space in our day and in our physical environment can help us feel more spacious and open.

MANTRA

WHAT

IS MY

INTENTION

RIGHT

NOW?

COME *Home* TO YOURSELF

No matter how far you travel and all the places you go throughout your day, you can come home to yourself at any time. Take a deep breath and bring your mind and body into the same place. Gently touching or lightly tapping your arms, legs, face, or shoulders can help you awaken the body, orient you to your environment, and create a moment of embodied presence.

Witching Hour MEDITATION

There's something about the hours of 4pm to 6pm that can derail even the most lovely of days. It's an unfortunate combination of hunger, a natural energy dip in the afternoon, and the emotional exhaustion of children who have been "on" and following rules all day. When you know the witching hour is approaching, take a deep breath and try to resource yourself with some quick self-care. As the fussing and fighting and whining begin, try to welcome them the way you welcome your emotions. "Oh, hello, cranky time. I see you are very punctual today." With a bit of humor, preparation, and detachment, you can use your own magic to transform the witching hours.

BE *Creative*

Make time today for something that's creative or artistic. Color or paint with your child, turn on some music and dance, write in a journal, work on a scrapbook, arrange some flowers, do some baking, or something else that gets your creative juices flowing! When we focus our attention on a creative task, we often enter a state of meditative absorption called "flow," which the research tells us is a very pleasurable state, and one that frees the mind to think in new ways.

MINDFUL *Reminders*

Create small reminders to cue you to check in with your attention throughout the day. You could place stickers or dots in places you'll see them every day—on the fridge, on your computer, or above the changing table. You could also make your cue a particular behavior that you do many times during the day—walking through a doorway, picking up your phone, turning off a light. When you see or "activate" your mindful reminder, just pause for a moment, and check in: What are you doing? Where's your attention? How do you feel? Is there anything you need?

MANTRA

WHERE IS MY ATTENTION RIGHT NOW?

A DAY OF *Kindness*

Make today a day of kindness. Create a special card to give to your child, write a note of gratitude to your partner or a good friend, or write down all the things you appreciate about yourself. See if you can offer kindness to strangers, too—a smile, a door held open, a sincere compliment ... no act is too small! Notice what it feels like to approach your day with kindness.

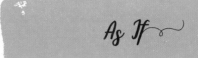

As If

In *The Power of Now*, author and spiritual teacher Eckhart Tolle writes, "Whatever the present moment contains, accept it as if you had chosen it." Can you bring this attitude to your day today? Can you greet every moment as if it were exactly as you would have designed it?

Mindful CLEANING

The repetitive movements of cleaning your home can be a soothing meditation if you choose to make them so. As you tidy up today, bring your awareness to the movements of your body. Notice the sights and smells and sounds around you. Take a moment to express gratitude for the spaces and objects you are cleaning. Your daily chores can be drudgery—or you can make them a special practice in caring for your home and protecting those who live in it with you. The choice is yours.

Waiting IN LINE MEDITATION

You probably spend a good portion of your day waiting in line. If you're like many of us modern mamas, you probably use that time to check email and social media. For today, pay attention to what you do when you're waiting in line—is there an urge to distract yourself with your phone? See what happens if you decide to be completely present with the experience of waiting in line. What if you engaged the cashier in conversation, played peek-a-boo with your child, or simply allowed yourself to pause and breathe?

ONE *Mindful* ACTIVITY

Choose one activity today that you will do with complete presence and attention. Try to pick something that you often do mind-*less*-ly, such as loading the dishwasher, preparing a bottle, folding the laundry, or walking to your desk at work. Pay attention to the movements of your body, your internal sensations, and the sounds and sights and smells around you. Notice what it's like to be completely present in very ordinary moments.

A Day OF NO COMPLAINING

Challenge yourself to an entire day of not complaining. Notice when the tendency arises to say what you don't like about something, or to state your wish that things were other than they are. Is there a different way you can approach the situation? Can you say something positive or constructive instead? This doesn't mean you have to go through your day saying "Everything is Awesome!" It's simply an invitation to notice how perseverating on the things we don't like can impact our day, and to experiment with a different way of being.

Slow DOWN

See if there is a part of your day that you can deliberately slow down. It might be washing the dishes or making lunches more slowly, or it could be walking at a more regular pace rather than speed walking to the store or to your place of work. You don't need to go obnoxiously slow—try to go about 70 percent of your regular speed. What does it feel like to slow down? If you're usually really fast (like most of us are), you might discover that it's actually quite normal and acceptable, and in fact a bit pleasanter, to move slightly less forcefully through the world. (If you find you prefer hurried movement, that's okay too. The point is to be mindful of what you do, no matter what your pace).

MANTRA

WHAT IS HAPPENING IN MY BODY RIGHT NOW?

MANTRA

I WILL

MOVE

THROUGH

MY DAY

WITH

AWARENESS

AND

ATTENTION.

I'M TOO DISTRACTED *to be Mindful!*

A lot of mothers tell me they could be mindful if only they didn't get interrupted all the time. But what if you saw all those distractions *as part of the practice*? What if you brought your mindful awareness to distraction? How do you feel in your body when interruptions occur? What thoughts arise? What *involuntary* responses do you typically enact (sighing, gritting your teeth, clenching your fists)? What *voluntary* responses emerge (complaining, getting upset, allowing)? In mindfulness, a distraction is not an obstacle to practice—it *is* the practice. We work with whatever arises.

BE *Still*

For one whole minute today, just be still. No movement, no noise. Just be still.

Breathe BEFORE YOU SPEAK

For today, try taking a full breath with awareness before you speak. It doesn't need to be an obvious, deep yogic breath; it's simply a way for you to bring yourself completely into this moment before you speak and engage with another person. It allows you to be completely present in your conversation, and supports meaningful communication and understanding.

Walking MEDITATION

Most of us walk simply as a means to an end—we have somewhere we need to be. Can you make walking an intentional activity today? As you walk, observe how your body moves and feels. Can you sense how your body moves as you take each step? Can you feel all the different muscles that engage in so many different ways as you do this complicated activity with ease every single day? Notice the sensations of placing your feet on the ground, attend to your breath and your heart rate, and take a look at the world (or gym) around you. Meditation doesn't always have to happen on your cushion. You can be mindful as you walk (and run and skip and tiptoe) through your day.

It's Okay TO LOVE THE TIMES WHEN YOU'RE AWAY

Sometimes mothers feel they must "confess" to me that they love it when they have the house to themselves, or when they go to work and have adult conversations for several hours, or even when they go to the grocery store by themselves. But this needn't be a *confession*— it's not a sin to cherish the time that's just for you. Someday your children will no longer need your daily care, and now is the time when it's important to nurture your own interests and your relationship with yourself so *you* are still fully here when that day arrives.

MANTRA

I CAN MAKE ANY MOMENT A MINDFUL MOMENT.

HOW DO YOU *Avoid?*

We all have our particular go-to strategies for avoiding unpleasant emotions or discomfort. Today, see if you can bring your attention to the ways you might distract yourself from your own experience—it might be something obvious like grabbing your phone or watching television, or it might be more subtle, like blaming others, getting angry, or explaining things away ("I'm just tired …"). When you notice these strategies, try to stay mindfully with your difficult experience, even if just for a few seconds. As you start to become more aware of your avoidance practices, you can ask yourself, "Am I doing this as a way to escape? Can I stay with this difficult moment instead?" You may discover that the discomfort is not as unbearable as it seems.

NOT NOW

One of my teachers says that "not now" is *always* an acceptable response to a difficult moment. We don't always have the emotional and mental bandwidth to process an intense experience, or we may not be in the right place for deep self-exploration (for example, when your toddler pitches a fit in the checkout line). In those moments, you can note what is arising, and say, "Not now." You're not suppressing your experience; you're recognizing it for what it is, and wisely intuiting that now is not the right time. If it's a BIG something that's arising, you can be pretty sure it will be back another time for you to work with it. So breathe, allow the experience to be as it is, and then reflect on the difficult moment when you have the time and space to do so.

Mindful
EXERCISE

Make your workouts mindful. Ditch the headphones and turn off the TV, and focus your attention on your amazing body and your powerful muscles and all the incredible things you can do with them. Make your exercise routine a true mind-body practice.

Transition Time

Some of the most challenging moments of your day are probably moments of transition—getting out the door in the morning, putting toys away, collecting the kids from school, or getting ready for bed. As with most challenges, your awareness and preparedness are crucially important. Create a routine where you ring a bell (either a real bell, or use an app with soothing meditation bells) to indicate that it's almost time to transition to something else. When the bell is rung, allow everyone to take a deep breath to prepare themselves. The bell is a much more gentle reminder than the verbal warnings (or threats) that you may be in the habit of giving in these stressful moments. See if taking a mindful pause makes the transition easier.

Stir THE Rice MINDFULLY

Mindfulness teacher Sharon Salzberg tells the story of a wise mother who was super-busy with many children, and yet was completely mindful and present. When asked how she had time to meditate with all those kids around, the woman explained that she simply stirred the rice mindfully. You may not have time for meditation today, or even tomorrow. But can you stir the rice mindfully? Can you make the lunches mindfully? Can you give your child a bath mindfully?

Standing
MEDITATION

Meditation is said to happen in four main postures: sitting, lying, walking, and standing. As so much of parenting is done literally on your feet, it can help to try a standing meditation. To do this (a great time is when you're waiting in line at the store), notice your feet grounding into the floor. Put down baskets or bags and slowly shift your weight from side to side, feeling the earth support you. Gently bend your knees, and tuck your pelvis in to reduce strain on your back. Roll your shoulders up and back and allow your arms to hang effortlessly at your side.

Who's Driving?

Throughout your day, ask yourself, "Who's driving?" Are you present and in control, making decisions with awareness and intention? Or has your auto-pilot taken over, leading you to make careless mistakes or be driven by habitual reactions? When you notice your inner chauffer has taken the wheel on a route she's not really equipped for, see if you can get yourself back in the driver's seat.

WHAT'S MY *Motivation*?

Try to get into the habit of checking in with your motivation for the actions you take. Every move has an intention behind it, whether we are aware of it or not. Is your question "What should we do today?" an invitation for everyone to share their input, or an attempt to steer them to *your* agenda? Today, practice noticing the brief moments *before* you act. Investigate what has prompted your desire to act, what thoughts you're having about what the outcome will be, and whether the action you are about to take is one that is necessary and helpful in that moment. You might be surprised by how many times you act without thinking, or how some behaviors may be prompted by unskillful motivations. This isn't about judging or criticizing yourself. Think of it as gathering data to help you cultivate the insight that will help you act the way you want to in the world.

Change IT UP

We are creatures of habit—every day we might eat the same breakfast, drive the same way to work, park in the same spot, and walk the same route with the dogs. It's not that habits are bad (indeed, having some things on auto-pilot frees up space in our head for more complicated activities). But habits can prevent us from engaging with our life with awareness. Today, see if you can change up a habit—brush your teeth with the opposite hand, sit in a different spot in your meeting, walk a different way to the park. See what you notice when you're not on auto-pilot.

Fab Five

The moment when everyone arrives home after school or after work can be a challenging time, so try implementing the "Fab Five." For the first five minutes when everyone is reunited, the focus is simply on connecting: hugs and kisses, how are yous and I missed yous. There's no opening the mail, rushing to make dinner, nagging about homework, checking email, or tidying the morning mess. There will be time for all that later; for the minutes of the "Fab Five," it's just about reconnecting with the ones you love.

ARE YOU *Pounding* THE PAVEMENT?

I mean that question literally—when you walk around during the day, do you pound the pavement, slamming your feet into the ground instead of lightly stepping on the earth? You can cause yourself all sorts of aches and pains when you walk with heavy legs and feet, which sends a jarring impact through your spine. Can you try walking softly today, imagining that your feet and legs are weightless as you bring them to the ground?

Making Dinner MEDITATION

If I had to guess one of the most challenging moments of your daily routine, I would bet it's dinnertime—you're trying to make a nutritious meal, there are things burning and boiling and needing your vigilant attention, and your children often choose this time to demand even more of your limited mental bandwidth. This is a perfect moment to remind yourself, "I am doing the best I can. It's normal for my child to want my attention, especially when I have to turn to something else. I am nourishing myself and my family with this meal, and I can handle some fussing in the background while I attend to the task at hand."

CHEST *Openers*

Chest openers are a great exercise for all of us, but especially nursing mothers. We spend much of our day hunched over a baby, a toddler, or a computer, and it takes a toll on our back. Often, we aren't even aware of the tension in our body until we collapse into bed, achy and exhausted. Simple exercises throughout the day can help us release these tensions. Try standing up and stretching your arms behind you, clasping your hands together if you can. Lift your head and chest and pull your shoulders back. Do these several times a day when you need a quick stretch.

CHAPTER 5

Support

MINDFULNESS FOR DIFFICULT MOMENTS

Raising little people is hard work, which means as a mother there will be no shortage of opportunities to practice working with difficulty. The meditations in the previous chapters are the practice for the stuff we need to deal with here: how to keep our cool when our children get fired up and start pushing buttons we didn't even know we had.

When these difficult moments arise, you have a choice: how are you going to be with them? Are you going to fight the difficulty? Are you going to kick and scream at it? Are you going to wish it away? Or are you going to allow it, get curious about it, and then see what happens in the next moment? The meditations and practices in this chapter will help you in doing the latter, so you can meet the hard parts of motherhood with greater ease.

WHAT DO I
Control?

Sometimes you can take refuge in Reinhold Neibuhr's
Serenity Prayer, which counsels us to change the things
we can change, and to accept the things we cannot. If you've
hit a tough moment, ask yourself, "What do I control?" There's a
lot you do not control—the weather, traffic, viruses, homework, or
your child's behavior, to name just a few. But in every moment,
there is at least something you *can* control—perhaps it's your
response, your attitude, or simply your breath. Take a deep breath,
and allow the things you don't control to be as they are. Take
another deep breath, and engage in wise action toward the
things you *do* control.

"I *Can* DO THIS"

As hard as things get during your day, remind
yourself, "I can do this." You've done hard
things before. You've tended wounds and
soothed tears and cleaned up the most nasty
of messes. Know that whatever it is you are
facing, you already have everything you need
to handle it. You have your presence, your
attention, and your breath. You've got this,
Mama. Repeat the mantra "I Can Do This."

MANTRA

MY

PRESENCE

IS ENOUGH.

WHAT'S *Arising* IN YOU?

Our children's behaviors usually provoke some kind of internal experience in us, and sometimes we end up reacting not to our *child's* behavior, but to whatever is arising in *our* mind and body. When you get triggered by your child today, pay attention to what comes up for you: bodily sensations, emotions such as anger or resentment, or perhaps memories from your own childhood or times you've experienced what your child is going through. Can you tell if your reaction is primarily to your child, or to your own issues that are arising? There's no need to judge yourself when your "stuff" comes up—just notice it. You can respond more effectively to your child's needs when you are able to separate them from your own.

MANTRA

I CAN

HANDLE THIS.

It's Okay NOT TO LOVE EVERY MINUTE OF IT

Well-meaning acquaintances often ask mothers, "Don't you just love every minute of it?" And while there is much to love about motherhood, it's hard to love every minute of it. Some parts—ugly tantrums, bedtime battles, potty training—are downright miserable, and thinking that you're supposed to be *loving* it only makes it worse. Whatever response you are having to the present moment is completely acceptable, *because it's the response you are having!* Just because things are difficult and uncomfortable right now doesn't mean that you don't love being a mother, or that you don't love your children—it just means it's hard right now.

Don't Cry OVER SPILLED MILK

When milk has spilled onto the kitchen floor, what is needed of you? You need to clean up the milk. You can't go back in time and unspill the milk. You can't yell at the milk (well, you can … but let me know how that goes). What you *can* do is clean up the milk. You can clean up the milk with anger and resentment, or you can clean up the milk with presence and without judgment. You can clean up the milk and let your mind go wild with irritating thoughts of how many more times you'll be cleaning up spilled milk and other fluids today. Or you can clean up the milk with thoughts about cleaning up this milk from this floor right now. The choice is yours.

Under THE SEA

It can help to think of a rough moment of your day as a stormy sea: the violent waves, heavy rain, and screaming thunder capture and almost overwhelm your attention. But if you were to dip below the surface, and peer down a little bit, you'd see that the bottom of the sea is perfectly cool and still. When the storms of your day assault the sense receptors at the top of your body, flooding your eyes and ears and the space between with sound and fury, see if you can drop down into your body, sensing your breath in your belly and your feet on the ground, and find some stillness under the sea.

"I am Enough"

You are enough. Your presence, your worries, your love, your mistakes, your hugs, your sorrys, your smiles, your tears, your kisses, your failures, your joy ... it's all enough. You don't need to be anyone or anything but you. Tell yourself, "I am enough."

Don't BAKE THE CAKE

Be mindful of what you can realistically achieve in the time you have available. You may decide to go all out and bake a Pinterest-worthy birthday cake for your child's party, complete with matching homemade decorations. But if in doing so you stress yourself out, and don't have enough time to wrap the presents, prepare the goodie bags, and clean the house, you'll just make yourself miserable. Be mindful of what you have the time and energy to do. Go ahead and *buy* a cake if you don't have time to bake the cake!

Begin AGAIN

Every moment of every day is a chance to make a fresh start. Each moment is an opportunity to pause, to apologize, to help, to listen. Each moment is an invitation to revisit your intentions and begin again.

Time-Outs AREN'T JUST FOR KIDS ANYMORE!

When things get really tense and heated, you can call a time-out for everyone—you, the kids, even the dog. A time-out isn't a punishment. It's a time to stop, step back from the intensity of a difficult moment, and breathe. When you sense everyone just needs a break today, call "Time out!" and allow everyone, including you, a chance to close their eyes and reset. (See the next chapter for soothing practices to do with your child in these time-outs.)

Overwhelm

Mothers constantly tell me they are overwhelmed. Mindfulness teacher Shinzen Young says that overwhelm is a "loss of sensory discrimination"—we become so flooded with sensations that we cannot separate or distinguish them. With mindful awareness, we cultivate the ability to break down our emotions into distinct sensory events. When you feel overwhelmed today, see if you can stop and identify the component parts of your experience. What bodily sensations are present? What's happening in your mind? Seeing the moment as a composition of various sensations, thoughts, memories, and judgments makes it much more manageable than a vague, but powerful, feeling of "overwhelm."

Story TIME

In her book *Rising Strong*, researcher Brené Brown suggests that we approach a difficult moment with, "The story I'm telling myself right now is …" Sometimes, we're telling the story of the hardworking mother whose children are ungrateful and whose spouse is unhelpful, and sometimes we're telling a story about all the other mothers who are judging us and thinking we're doing a terrible job at parenting. It's helpful to take a look at the stories you are telling yourself throughout the day. Are they true? Are they helpful? If those stories weren't there, what would be?

If Only …

How often during the day do our thoughts turn to "If only …"? "If only he were a bit older," "If only I weren't so tired," "If only she could nap longer." Well, things are only as they are … and we add to our suffering when we keep wishing they were somehow different. For today, pay attention to the times when you are hoping for something *other* than what is happening—when you are wishing your child were different, or you were different, or your house were different. You don't need to get upset with yourself for thinking this way (we all do it!)—just notice this common habit of our minds. When you notice these thoughts, pay attention to how they make you feel, and ask yourself, "Can I accept this moment, this child, this house, this me, exactly as it is, right here and right now?"

MANTRA

WHAT CAN I LEARN FROM THIS?

WHAT DO I *Need?*

As mothers, we often put everyone else's needs ahead of our own, and it's difficult even to think to ask, "What do *I* need?" Take a moment today to consider your needs: Do you need more sleep? Do you need more help at home or at work? Do you need 10 minutes to yourself? Do you need to take five deep breaths? Whatever it is you need, don't be afraid to name it and claim it.

ALL THE OTHER *Mothers*

If you are struggling with something today, you can guarantee that another mother is struggling with it, too. Throughout history, women have faced the daunting task of nurturing little people and helping them become competent big people. You may not see the other mothers today, but you share a bond with them that stretches for millennia. What you are struggling with, they have struggled with. Your struggles are part of the human condition, which means they are normal, universal, and completely deal-with-able.

Learning FROM A DIFFICULT MOMENT

After a difficult experience with your child, you may just want to forget about it and move on. But you can bring your mindful, nonjudgmental awareness to the encounter, reviewing what happened just *before* things went downhill. How were you feeling physically: Hungry, tired, or rested? How were you feeling emotionally? What were you thinking about? Were you present? Can you replay the moment and identify the specific behavior or incident that "triggered" you? How did it make you feel? What was happening in your body? What thoughts arose? *Can you identify the moment when you could have chosen to respond in a different way?* This isn't about blaming yourself—it's about becoming familiar with the things that upset you, and how you react. It's about locating those small, choice-full moments—even retroactively—so you can handle a similar situation differently the next time.

HELLO, ANXIETY

One of the most powerful mindfulness practices is to greet our emotions. The poet Rumi said we should invite our emotions into our lives as welcome guests. When I feel frustration or irritation or anxiety, I sometimes smile and say to myself (in a silent, though booming, inner voice), "Hello, Anxiety!" It sounds silly, but it works. Sometimes I'll say, "Thank you for coming by and reminding me of all the things I need to do, but I've got this." Today, try greeting your emotions by name. Thank them for the information they are providing you!

Feel YOUR *Feels*

Whatever you are feeling right now, truly *feel* it. Notice the sensations in your body—is there tightness or softness, warmth or coolness? Bring your attention to your thoughts, to any desires to take action, and see if you can identify what you are feeling. Research shows that suppressing emotions causes greater stress than experiencing them. And, as intense as it may be, an emotion usually lasts only about 90 seconds. Once the emotion has begun, you're on the ride, so see if you can stay with it, observe it, feel it, and watch it subside.

HOLD *Space*

When your child is having a difficult time, he needs you to hold space for him. Holding space for another person means we allow that person to have the experience he is having, without judgment, and without running away. We let him know that we can handle this difficulty together. When your child gets frustrated that he can't tie his shoes fast enough, you might be tempted to leave him "until he can do it without whining." What if, instead, you held space for him by being a calm presence next to him, offering encouragement with your words or simply your relaxed nervous system? When he sees you can tolerate frustration, he can begin to learn to tolerate it, too.

In the same way, when your child is fired up, he doesn't really need your words, he needs your stable, attuned presence. See if you can resist the urge to lecture, to explain that this isn't a big deal, or describe how he could be handling things better. Just stay with him, offering a hug or a soft touch if he will allow it. If he's too fired up to let you get close, stay near to him and breathe slowly (perhaps exaggerating your deep breaths as a demonstration). Your stable, non-judging presence is usually the most helpful thing you can offer.

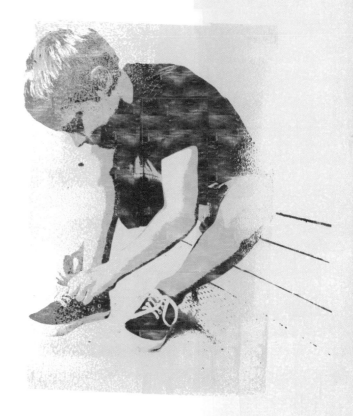

WHAT IS *Actually* HAPPENING?

With mindfulness, we learn to see the world with clarity, identifying what is actually happening in the present moment, as opposed to getting completely wrapped up in all our stories and worries. At any moment, you can ask yourself, "What is *actually* happening?" Although your mind may be busily creating a story about a willful and stubborn child who *always* acts this way, if you focus solely on *what is actually happening in this moment*, you can see a single tantrum as *just a tantrum*. And then you can respond more effectively to the needs of this present moment.

Children WILL BE CHILDISH

Sometimes I just need to remind myself that. It's simply in the nature of a one-year-old to make a mess and play loudly. It's in the nature of a four-year-old to move slowly, and sometimes clumsily. It's in the nature of a seven-year-old to find bodily functions humorous. Instead of getting frustrated that this little person does not yet act like an adult, see if you can find something to celebrate about who he is *now*, and treasure his child-ness. For tomorrow he'll already be a little bit older.

MANTRA

I DON'T
LIKE THIS,
BUT I CAN
BE WITH IT.

DON'T RESIST

When your day doesn't go according to plan, you have two choices: resist, or go with it. So often, our first instinct is to resist ("I don't want it to be this way," "I wanted this to happen instead.") But resisting what is happening—resisting the present moment—is exhausting, and it usually just makes things worse. When your day gets derailed, take a deep breath, and instead of fighting the present moment, see if you can soften into it. You don't have to *like* it, but it is here. Don't resist.

"IT'S HARD RIGHT NOW, *and That's Okay*"

Being a mother isn't always easy. Sometimes it's really hard. When you have a rough day, simply say to yourself, "It's hard right now, and that's okay." Just acknowledging that things are tough will make you feel better. You can even ask, "What do I need to do to take care of myself during this challenging time?" Whatever you are experiencing is completely normal … because it's what you are experiencing! You don't need to try to talk yourself out of how you are feeling. Simply say to yourself, "Sometimes it's hard, and that's okay."

WORK FROM THE *Bottom* TO THE *Top*

When you're really stressed out, it can be hard to access the mental bandwidth to use strategies such as reframing a crisis into an opportunity or investigating the needs behind your emotions. So start at the bottom: breathe, move your body a bit, sit up a bit taller, and just focus on being present with your breath. Pay attention to your body as you begin to activate your natural calming response (you can use the practices from Chapter 1 to do this).

Once you've soothed your body's stress response and brought your thinking back online, you can use your go-to cognitive strategies to meet your stress. You can reflect on the times in the past when you've handled something similar, you can practice reframing (see page 108), consider what you can learn from this moment (see pages 100 and 119), or find meaning in a difficult situation (see page 117).

DEALING WITH STRESS

"Top Down" Practices

MEANING:
Is there something I can learn from this?

REFRAME:
Is there another way to look at this?

MEMORY:
How have I dealt with this in the past?

"Bottom Up" Practices

BREATHE:
Breathe from the belly.
Lengthen the exhale.

EMBODY:
Sit up.
Move.
Exercise.

THIS CHILD, THIS MOMENT

When your child is having one of *those* moments, your only task is to parent *this* child in *this* moment. While your thoughts might drift to all the other times she's behaved in this way, or all the times she may do so in the future, all you can respond to right now is *this behavior* from *this child* in *this moment*. It doesn't mean you can't address the underlying issues later, but right now, just focus *on this moment*, instead of all of *those moments*.

YOU GET *to Choose*

In any given moment, you can choose your:
- Attitude
- Words
- Actions

It's an incredible power. Choose joyfully, with presence and wisdom.

MISBEHAVIOR IS *an Invitation*

With mindful awareness and patience, we can see our child's misbehavior as an invitation. It's an invitation to consider what our child needs in this moment. Most kids know how they're *supposed* to behave, and they generally *want* to behave in that way, so when that behavior doesn't happen, it's an invitation for us to be curious. What need of hers is not being met? Does she need attention, rest, food, water, a hug? Does she know? Accept the invitation, and find out.

YOUR LIFE IS *Real*

You'll drive yourself crazy comparing yourself to the mothers in magazines or in your Pinterest feed. There's no one perfect way to mother, and your child will develop according to his own timeline, not the one outlined in a parenting article. Advertisements and social media are not intended to be a reflection of reality and shouldn't be taken as such. Be mindful of staying in *your* reality, and resist comparing yourself, your parenting skills, and your child to anyone else.

Everyone's HARD IS HARD

It's tempting to try to talk yourself out of feeling upset when there are people who are in much worse situations than you are all over the globe. But you know what? *Everyone's hard is hard.* If it's hard for you, then it's hard. You needn't feel guilty for acknowledging your own pain and difficulty; in fact, that's how you will strengthen yourself so that you may help others.

IT GETS *Better*

If there's one thing I know for certain from my own motherhood experience, it's that *it gets better.* The sleepless nights don't last forever, the battles over naps and potty-training will one day be a distant memory, and eventually this helpless little tot will be able to feed and dress herself … and even drive! As she gets older and you get wiser and you both get to know each other better, things may not necessarily get *easier*, but they do get a lot better.

Some Days ARE JUST NOT HAPPY DAYS

Mindfulness is not going to make us happy all the time (nor, really, would we want it to). Some days, honestly, are just miserable—the kids are cranky, we're cranky, and nothing turns out as we expected. That's just how some days are. Please don't put pressure on yourself to be smiling and happy every day. If it's a hard day, just sit with your hard day. It's okay, and it won't last.

It's Okay TO BE WRONG

No one—not even your children—expects you to have all the answers and always to get it right. It's okay not to know the solutions to the homework. It's okay to make mistakes. We all do. It's okay to realize you could have done it better. Remember that we want our children to know it's okay to get things wrong sometimes, and we should extend that same kindness and leniency to ourselves.

Forgiveness MEDITATION

If you are struggling with your feelings of being hurt by someone, see if you can practice a silent forgiveness meditation. Bring to mind the person you want or need to forgive—it may be your child, your partner, a friend, or even yourself. Notice any negative judgments or thoughts that arise. Silently say to this person, "I forgive you. If you could have done better, in that moment, you would have."

Forgiving someone doesn't mean you are condoning what she did or releasing her from the consequences of her action. It means you are releasing *yourself* from resentment and anger. Forgiveness can be a difficult practice, and it may help to repeat this exercise a few times.

MANTRA

IF IT'S HARD FOR ME, IT'S HARD FOR OTHER MOTHERS, TOO.

Reframing

Psychologists tell us that many of our problems can become less overwhelming if we can reframe them, for there are many vantage points from which a situation can be viewed. When you're stuck in resentment or worry or frustration, ask yourself if you can put this scenario in a different frame. Is this child willful and stubborn, or is he passionate and confident? Is this another half hour of drudgery in the kitchen, or an opportunity to nurture your family's physical and emotional health through a home-made meal? The choice is yours.

THEY ARE NOT
Their Tantrums

A tough truth about motherhood is that the times when our children most need our loving attention and support are the times when their behaviors are the least likely to evoke tenderness in us. A child throwing a tantrum needs your presence, and it can be easier to offer it if you remind yourself that "My child is not her tantrum." The tantrum is an outward manifestation of the big emotions her little body is struggling to process. Can you see the sweet child beneath the surface behavior? Can you hold space with her (see page 101) as this storm passes through her?

"I AM DOING THE
Important Work"

Mothers often tell me that one of their biggest frustrations is feeling like they have nothing to show for all the work they do. But mindfulness is about not attaching to outcomes: we do something because it is meaningful or necessary, without holding tightly to an expected result. And that's a lot of what motherhood is! Mothering cannot be measured in profit and loss charts or tallies of widgets made. The important work of mothering is mothering itself: the tending and feeding and singing and hugging and redirecting and bathing and teaching and laughing and boo-boo kissing. You are doing the important work, Mama, so tell yourself that!

IT'S THE *Hormones*

I'm talking about your teen, not you. It can be difficult to watch your sweet child transition into a moody and unpredictable tween. As best you can, try to remember yourself at that age, with a changing body and fluctuating hormones and a more challenging social world. When your tween or teen starts acting all teenager-y, remind yourself that "It's the hormones." It's a normal process as your child begins to assert her independence and make sense of a stage of development that's challenging for everyone.

TANTRUM *Meditation*

If we could rank mindfulness practices from *beginner* to *total ninja*, staying mindfully calm and present during a loud, screaming tantrum would absolutely qualify you for a black belt. If tantrums trigger you, welcome to the club! The next time your child starts firing on all cylinders, see if you can act as the brakes. First, take a deep breath and ground yourself by feeling your feet, noticing how they anchor you in place. Allow that to be the stable base you stand on, projecting calm and presence as your child rages; this lets your child know that you can handle this moment, even if she cannot. As best you can, see if you can observe the tantrum not as the parent trying to "fix" it, but as an outsider.

Be curious about the tantrum: Can you identify the need your child is trying to meet? Can you identify the moment the tantrum "peaks," when your child's energy shifts and she is ready to hear your soothing and comforting voice? As with any training, the Tantrum Meditation takes practice, but over time see if you notice yourself being less reactive and more intentionally aware during these difficult parenting moments. Notice the impact your presence has on your child.

THIS, TOO, SHALL *Pass*

My mother said this to me many times
when my children were younger and
going through difficult stages. It helped
me remember that no emotion, phase,
or pain lasts forever. Sometimes the
ever-changing and shifting nature of
the world is a challenge, and
sometimes we can take comfort
in the impermanent nature
of our experience.

RESENTMENT

Resentment may be one of the most
difficult experiences for us to work
with as mothers, because it can lead
to intense feelings of guilt. But it is a
completely normal and quite common
feeling—our children demand so
much of us, and it can be incredibly
overwhelming at times. We may long
for our easy, kid-free days, or wish that
everything would just be quiet, or we
might miss the independence we once
had. When resentment arises, be
compassionate with yourself. Can you
sense what need of yours is not being
met? Do you know what you could do
to meet that need?

ALL THE *Terrible* THINGS

Mark Twain supposedly once quipped, "I've
been through a lot of terrible things in my life,
some of which actually happened." Can you
notice the times when *you* allow yourself to
get completely caught up in the drama and
trauma of an event that is not actually
happening? When you catch yourself doing
this, see if you can remember Twain's mocking
words, and remind yourself to focus on what is
actually happening.

IT *IS* A BIG DEAL

Sometimes we tell our children to stop crying, stop worrying, or stop fussing because "it isn't a big deal." What we often forget is that when you're little, *everything* is a big deal. When you live so entirely in the moment, playing Lego means the whole world becomes Lego. If the Lego structure collapses, it's a *really big deal.* When your child gets upset today, draw upon your empathy and see the situation from his perspective. Let him know you understand that this is a big deal to him, and that you "get" his frustration.

"I AM NOT MY ANGER"

When we say, "I am angry," it's almost as if we become anger itself; we completely identify with this emotion and it takes over our entire experience. With mindfulness, we try to see an emotion as something that arises within us; we notice that anger is present, not that we "are" angry. When a difficult emotion arises today, tell yourself, "I am not this emotion." You are not sadness, or fear, or jealousy, or any other single component of your experience—you contain multitudes! You are the awareness that holds all that is happening within you, including your emotional experiences. See if you can observe the emotion objectively, rather than identifying with it. Taking this more detached stance toward emotions can help you respond more skillfully in a difficult moment.

DON'T TAKE IT *Personally*

Motherhood is an incredibly personal act, but sometimes we need not to take it so personally. When your child is upset, or misbehaving, or otherwise acting unskillfully, it's usually not about you. Even when she tells you you're the worst mother in the world, it's still not really about you. Her young mind and little body are dealing with big emotions and complicated rules, which can provoke all sorts of unskillful words and behaviors. There will be time later, when she has calmed down, that you can talk about behaviors and consequences, but for now, don't take it personally. Right now, she needs you to be the safe container to help her hold this difficult experience.

Charming CHATTERBOX

Little kids like to tell stories, often the *same* stories, over and over and over again. There may be days when you just want your little chatterbox to get to the point and wrap it up so you can have a few moments of silence. When this happens, notice your irritation and see if you can summon the patience for another round of "the cool world I just built in Minecraft." Your child wants to share his world and his ideas with you. Can you see the charm in your chatterbox? Can you appreciate that one day, he may not be so chatty, and you might miss these moments?

MANTRA

I ACCEPT.

SHUN THE *"Shoulds"*

One word we can get stuck on is "should": I *should* be doing this, I *should* be doing that. With all the pressure to multitask, it's easy to convince yourself that you *should* be doing something *more* than what you're doing right now. Remind yourself that you are most effective when you are doing one thing at a time. If it helps, you can keep a "should list" nearby so you can jot down the activities that must be attended to later; then you can return your attention to the present moment and the task at hand.

THE WORST MOTHER *in the World*

You, too? My daughter first screamed this universal epithet at me when she was about six years old, and I was completely taken aback. My subsequent pause may have been more out of shock than intentional mindfulness. But this incident taught me that when our children "talk back," our best response is usually to, well, not talk back. I truly believe that our children want to do and say the right thing most of the time, and if we just give them a bit of space to hear their words land, to observe our nonverbal reaction to those words and consider what they said, they'll realize pretty quickly that they didn't mean it. In this particular case, my daughter paused and then said, "Well, actually, you're not the worst mother in the world … I'm just mad at you." I know you're not the worst mother in the world, and your child knows it too. She may just need a brief pause to figure it all out.

WATCH OUT FOR THE
"Always"

The word "always" tends to creep into our mental chatter in difficult moments. "They *always* act this way!" "He's *always* late." Today, watch out for "always." It's a seductive mind-trap that can fuel and intensify your anger. But "always" is rarely right! When "always" enters your thoughts today, take a moment to ask, "Really? *Always?*"

HOW DO YOU
Handle STRESS?

We all have different ways of managing stress. For the next few days, keep track of the things you do when you get stressed out or overwhelmed—write down the little responses, such as sighing or gritting your teeth, as well as the more time-consuming ones, such as reaching for your phone, exercising, napping, or eating junk food. After a few days, consider your list and think about which of your stress responses are working for you, and which ones aren't. Which ones are soothing or energizing, and which ones are agitating or draining? Which ones do you need more of? Are there any that you need less of?

Narrate YOUR PRACTICE

When you feel you're about to "lose it" in front of your kids, pause and take a deep breath, and narrate the mindful strategies you are using. "I'm feeling really frustrated right now, so I'm going to stop and take five deep breaths." You can even exaggerate the breaths, or breathe loudly, to make them obvious to your children. "Breathing like this helps me calm down so I can deal with what's happening without getting really mad or doing something I'll feel bad about later." If you can give voice to your emotions and experience, it will help you calm down, and it's a powerful way to model mindfulness practice for your children.

FIND THE *Yes* IN THE NO

If children are masters at uttering one word, it's "no." And that one word can trigger mothers like no other. But when your child says "no" to something, he's also saying "yes" to something else. A "no" to cleaning up toys is perhaps a "yes" to more playtime. You don't have to indulge your child's defiance, but you can be mindful of your child's needs in this moment. Instead of fighting back with a "Yes, you *will* clean up your toys," you can say, "We'll have more time for playing cars after dinner, but right now we need to clean up for lunch." For today, determine what your child is saying "yes" to when he says "no," and see if it helps to diffuse tense moments.

This, TOO

When you hit a difficult moment, see if you can welcome it with, "This, too." This, too, is part of your experience. This, too, is something that can be held in your gentle awareness. This, too, may not be pleasant, but you can be with it.

MANTRA

I WILL CHOOSE TO SEE IT THIS WAY INSTEAD.

MEANING

Psychiatrist and Holocaust survivor Victor Frankl has said that "suffering ceases to be suffering at the moment it finds a meaning." When things are hard, can you find the meaning? Is there a lesson to be learned, a new direction to be explored? The meaning of a particularly difficult time in your life may not be readily apparent, but you can probably think of harrowing times in your past that helped shape you into who you are today. Can you trust that if the meaning is not discernible right now, it will be some day?

You Don't Have to
ADDRESS EVERY INFRACTION

The pressure to raise a perfectly well-behaved child can turn us into the discipline police, ready to take action on any and all infractions. But this will completely drain all your energy by 8am if you make it your default mode. You are the sheriff in this town, and you get to decide which behaviors warrant an investigation. Some sibling arguments are best resolved by the kids themselves. Sometimes your child will confess his wrongdoing before you need to address it. Some comments are made provocatively, purely to see if you'll take the bait. There's much we don't control in motherhood, but we *do* get to pick our battles. Choose yours wisely.

WHAT'S THE *Diagnosis?*

In *The Courage to Teach*, educator Parker Palmer reminds teachers that "the way we diagnose our students' condition will determine the kind of remedy we offer." The same goes for parents: if you diagnose your child as stubborn, or manipulative, or lazy, that will determine the help you offer and how you respond to her behavior. If she's hungry, but you've concluded she has a "bad attitude," you may administer the wrong medicine (a lecture instead of an apple). For today, notice the times when you are prematurely diagnosing your child. Channel your inner doctor and carefully consider the symptoms your child presents, cultivating a curious bedside manner and asking your child if you've understood her condition and her needs. The more accurate your diagnosis, the better the prognosis.

"I WON'T *Always* TRY TO FIX IT"

When your child is really upset, what she needs is *not* your answers, your fixing, your moralizing, or your stories. What she needs is your permission to have her experience. She wants and needs you to hear her words with presence and empathy. She needs the safe space to feel what she's feeling. In these moments, what she needs from you is complete, silent, whole-body listening, without judgment, questioning, or advice. She simply needs you to meet her where she's at with empathy. (See also Allow Silence on page 123.) So however hard it is to hold back, tell yourself you're not going to try to fix it today.

"NOW IT'S OKAY"

When a difficult moment comes to an end, help calm your body's stress response by telling yourself, "Now it's okay." The baby wouldn't sleep, but now it's okay. The children were fighting, the house was a mess, the day felt way too crazy, but now it's okay.

Insight MEDITATION

Mindfulness meditation is sometimes called "insight meditation," which is a perfect description of the practice: we pay attention in order to cultivate insight and wisdom. Through carefully attending to your experience, you may discover that you hit the same problems every week. Think of this as an invitation to consider possible solutions. Can homework be done at a different time of the afternoon? If your child is resisting going to dance lessons, is it time to call it quits and find an activity that better meets her interests? When you start to see all your experiences as data, you can figure out what's working, what's NOT working, and find new solutions.

Loving Kindness
FOR YOUR CHILD

This meditation can be really helpful to do on a day—or during a phase—that is difficult for you and your child. Take a deep breath, and bring an image of your child to your mind. Really picture him—what's he doing, what's he wearing, what's the expression on his face? Place your hands on your heart, and silently repeat the following phrases to yourself, imagining that you are sending these wishes straight to your child:

May you be happy
May you be safe
May you be healthy
May you be loved

Take another deep breath and notice what it feels like to send these kind thoughts to your child.

CHAPTER 6

Together Time

MINDFULNESS WITH YOUR KIDS

Adults who discover the practice of mindfulness quickly recognize that it would have been a powerful tool to have as a kid. The most effective way you can teach your children mindfulness is by example. Through your calm presence, deliberate pauses, carefully chosen words, and genuine empathy, you will model what it means to pay attention with love and curiosity.

Right now, you may just want to focus on your own practice, and that's totally okay. It's important that you feel comfortable with mindfulness before you try to teach it to your kids. When you're ready, you'll find that teaching mindfulness strategies to your children will help them be more focused and attentive, and will help them better understand and regulate their emotions. You can get started with the suggestions and games provided here.

JUST *Hug*

When we give and receive hugs, our body releases oxytocin, a hormone that promotes bonding and trust. This makes us feel good and relaxed. So give your child a hug, or even give yourself a hug! (Your neurons don't know it's you, so you'll still get a juicy dose of happy hormones if the hug comes from you.)

THE 300TH ROUND OF *Candyland*

You've probably played Candyland (or trucks or Barbies) at least 300 times. It's easy to grow weary of it. But you've never played on *this* day, with *this* child, who is just a little bit different from the way she was yesterday. So *play*. Notice your child's face and words and actions. Be present. You'll never play this 300th round of Candyland again.

JUST TRYING TO GET *My Attention*

Sometimes we say that when a child is misbehaving, they are "just trying to get my attention." And we're right—they want our attention. They *need* our attention. As Zen teacher John Tarrant says, "attention is the most basic form of love." We show our children how much they mean to us and how special they are by giving them our undivided and loving attention. This doesn't mean they need 100 percent of our attention 100 percent of the time—that's neither healthy nor possible. But their need for our attention is primal and powerful. Be mindful of giving your child your loving attention throughout your day.

It's Hard TO FOLLOW RULES *All Day*

From the moment our children enter preschool, they are following rules and "holding it together" for a long time every day. When they get home, it's natural for tears, frustration, attitude, and misbehavior to "leak" out, after being contained all day. In some ways, at-home meltdowns are a good thing—they are a sign of our children's absolute faith in us, their confidence that we will stick by them no matter how messy things get. When things get rough after school, repeat the mantra "It's Hard to Follow the Rules All Day," and cultivate some empathy for your child.

It's Okay TO BE BORED

Perhaps nothing is so dreaded as your child complaining, "I'm *bored*." Notice the reaction that this statement creates in you—do you feel an urgent need to "fix" his boredom? Learning to tolerate boredom is an important skill for children to develop, for it's in moments of *not* filling time that creativity and problem-solving skills can be developed. When your child tells you he's bored, you can tell him, "It's okay to be bored." You can even ask him to get curious about his boredom: How do you know you're bored? What does boredom feel like? Boredom is not a problem to be solved; it's an invitation to be creative.

MANTRA

I CAN CHOOSE MY ACTIONS AND MY BELIEFS.

Free Time

My children and I like to have "free time"—we set aside several hours on a weekend when I have to say "Yes" to everything they ask to do that is 1) screen-free and 2) actually free. (And, I did have to add later, *legal*.) We play board games, bake cookies, make crafts, read books, take naps, or walk the dogs. Without the distraction of screens or worries about expensive outings, we can be completely present with each other as we enjoy some simple pleasures.

Allow SILENCE

When you are with your child, and the conversation stalls, see if you can allow the silence. Your natural tendency may be to fill the moment with more talk and activity, but often the quiet serves as an invitation for your child to open up. This can be especially powerful when you are helping your child through a difficult situation. Instead of immediately trying to "fix" things, if you sit in silence and see what emerges, you might find that your child opens up to you and that you learn a lot more from her.

BE IN THE MOMENT *with your Child*

I remember one night when my son was aged four, and I was feeling particularly impatient about getting him to bed. He was moving too slowly for my agenda, and I noticed my irritation and the stories in my head: "He's always dawdling. I just want some time to myself and he's purposely stalling." Remembering to be mindful, I took a deep breath and really looked at him. I watched him play with how he could stretch his legs as he put on his pajamas, listened to him sing a gentle "loo-la-da-di-dahh …" as he readied himself for bed, and observed him curiously studying a small imperfection in the carpet by his tiny feet. He was totally and completely in the moment, mindful of his body and his surroundings. With mindfulness, I was able to join him in this precious moment.

Happy Days

Make a list with your kids of the things you can do as a family that make you happy—going to the movies, coloring together, snuggling on the couch, going for a walk, playing a game. On a day when not much is scheduled, declare a "Happy Day!" Each person in the family gets to pick one item on the list for everyone to do together. If you'd like, you can talk about why these things feel good.

BE MINDFUL *for* YOUR KIDS

Children have a hard time identifying their emotions. You can bring *your* mindful awareness to *their* experience by naming what is present. For example, when your child is getting upset, you could say, "It looks like you're feeling frustrated because Amy said she didn't want to share her doll with you. I bet you wish you two could play with it together." When you do this, you not only show empathy, but you help your child understand her emotions, needs, and desires in a way that she might not be able to verbalize yet.

READING *Mindfully*

Story time can be a great opportunity to have conversations about difficult emotions and experiences because your children can talk about the problems of *fictional characters,* instead of diving into their own messy and complicated feelings. They might even get some clarity or better understanding of their own experience by reflecting on the stories you read. You can ask your child questions such as, "Why do you think the boy is feeling sad?" "What do you think made the bunny so angry?" These questions can open up a powerful dialogue with your kids about emotions, behavior, and motivations.

Family Gratitude JOURNAL

Get a special notebook to keep in the kitchen or somewhere everyone will be able to find it, and make it a Family Gratitude Journal. Anyone can write in it about what they are thankful for. It's especially sweet to encourage your children to write down the nice things that other family members do for them, or what they appreciate about their family. Set aside some special nights during the year to read through the family journal.

NO-PHONE *Zone*

If you're in the habit of carrying your phone around the house with you, see if you can make bedtime a "no-phone zone." It's hard to be mindful and in the moment during bathtime, story time, and cuddle time with a buzzing phone constantly interrupting you. While you're at it, see if you can make *your* bedtime routine a no-phone zone— you'll rest a lot better at night if you're not stimulating your mind with brightly lit news and emails right before bed.

Silence ISN'T SILENT

Sit with your child and set a timer for 30 seconds. Tell your child that you are both going to be as quiet as possible for 30 seconds (you can try to make it a challenge if you think that will be hard for your little one!), and you are going to listen to all the sounds around you while you are silent. After the timer goes off, see if you can identify five things you heard. This gives your child practice in paying attention, and also gives him a taste of quiet stillness.

Namaste

This traditional greeting at the end of yoga classes is often translated as "the divine in me bows to (or honors) the divine in you." (You can use the phrase "the light in me" if you don't like the word "divine".) I think this is a beautiful phrase to introduce to our children. Namaste means we are all made of the same brilliant and radiant star stuff. Namaste means that when you hurt, I hurt, and when you are joyful, I am joyful. Namaste reminds us that we are all sentient, loving, and lovable creatures, no matter how much our outward behavior may obscure our inner light. Perhaps the next time your child throws a tantrum or yells at her sibling, you could say "Namaste" as a reminder that you know her behavior doesn't define who she is inside. You could encourage your kids to use this mantra to help them understand that other children—despite their behaviors—are just like they are inside.

I CAN TAKE MY FAMILY'S LOVE WITH ME THROUGHOUT MY DAY.

Mindful STORY TIME

You might be dreadfully exhausted when evening story time rolls around. This sometimes leads to inattention and frustration during what could be a sweet and tender closing moment for your day with your child. Tonight, bring your awareness to story time. Notice when your attention wanders, when your mouth is saying the words but your mind is miles away, thinking of to-do lists and upcoming meetings. See if you can bring your attention back to your body, back to sitting on this bed, back to the story, and back to your child.

Bedtime BODY SCAN

This is a really helpful practice for a child who is having trouble falling asleep at night. Invite him to lie down on his back in bed, and imagine that there is a soothing, softly glowing light down by his feet. Ask him to imagine that this light provides a safe and soothing warmth as it moves gently over his body. While the light is at his feet, have him sense his feet and allow them to relax, gently letting the feet spread apart as this light protects them. Then ask him to envision the light slowly traveling up his legs, to his knees, thighs, and hips. As the light comes over his belly, it helps him soften his upper body and breathe slowly and deeply. Continue bringing the light all the way up his torso, arms, neck, and face. This gentle light can envelop his body as he sleeps safely through the night.

Dance PARTY

Put on some fun tunes and bust a move with your kids. Turn up the volume, sing along to the music, and dance your heart out. It's great exercise, and dance is a powerful way to bring your mind and body into the same place as you move in sync with the sounds around you.

MY *Amazing* EMOTIONS

It's hard to watch our children struggle with big emotions, but there are ways we can help them process and begin to understand their own feelings. Depending on your child's age, when she is grappling with a difficult emotion, you can ask her questions such as: What color is this feeling? What does it look like? Does it have a name? What kind of animal would it be? What is the animal doing? You can invite younger kids to act out the animal/emotion, which can provide some relief from the overwhelming physical sensations of the feeling, and also help them get a better sense of what exactly they're experiencing. With older kids, you can ask questions such as: What kind of action does it feel like your body wants to take? If you could give a label to this emotion, what would it be?

THE TRAIN OF *Thought*

In the delightful Pixar movie *Inside Out*, the human mind is shown as literally having a "train of thought." This is a great visual representation of how thoughts run through the mind. If you have a toy train (preferably one with multiple cars), use that to demonstrate to your child how thoughts can move fast or slow, can be big or little, and can be colorful or dark. Tell your child to imagine that when she notices her thoughts, she is just watching a train go by with lots of ideas and words packed into the cars. She doesn't have to ride the train and get carried away by her thoughts; she can just watch it go by.

Dynamite!

This practice comes entirely from my son. When he was aged six, he put together a bundle of dynamite sticks made out of construction paper. If he got really upset about something, he would grab his fake dynamite sticks as he sensed his anger rising, and then he'd breathe as he gently relaxed his hold on the dynamite. He would allow the bundle to fall to the ground as he released his anger. Ask your child what *his* anger looks or feels like: Dynamite? A fist? A lion? A tornado? Have him craft a representation of his anger that he can use to visualize the process of holding his emotional experience and then loosening his grip on it.

COOKING *Together*

One way to beat the dinner-time craziness is to invite your children to help you. Depending on their ages, your children can set the table, stir ingredients, measure ingredients, or read the recipe to you. Cooking is an activity that engages all the senses—sight, smell, touch, hearing, and taste; you can talk with your children about all the sensory elements involved in making dinner.

SIMON SAYS

This traditional childhood game actually teaches children several important attentional skills: the ability to understand rules and adjust their behavior when the rules change; the ability to focus their concentration on a single task; the ability to control impulses; and the ability to hold information in working memory. Who knew?! You can make Simon Says easy or complicated based on the ages of your kids, but the premise is simple: the person playing Simon gives instructions ("touch your head," "turn in a circle," etc.), but the players do the action only if he says *"Simon says* touch your head." When kids get it wrong, use the mistake as an opportunity to talk about how hard it is *not* to act when we're given an instruction, and how we need to inhibit that impulse. You can also change the rules from time to time. ("Now we do the action if he *doesn't* say Simon says!") Have fun with it!

Music JAM

Gather your musical instruments, or simply find items around the house that can make some noise (you can drum with pencils, tap glasses with spoons, pluck rubber bands, or shake some spice jars). Have one person start a rhythm, and then ask everyone else to join in when they're ready. This is a fun game, and also a powerful way to attune to others by getting in sync with their sounds and movements. And you can create some amazing tunes in your free-flowing jam.

Neighborhood SCAVENGER HUNT

Practice mindfulness of your surroundings by taking your child on a scavenger hunt in your neighborhood. Set her some fun challenges: Does she know the color of the house three doors down? Can she find a house with 10 windows? How many houses are actually on your block? Is there a tree in everyone's yard? Can she find five things she's never noticed before about where you live?

"IT'S *Just* MINI-GOLF"

The first time I took my children mini-golfing was a disaster. Of course I imagined it would be idyllic fun—the kids and I would navigate windmills and toadstools and all sorts of brightly colored obstacles on a sunny day, while learning a little bit of hand-eye coordination along the way. But I managed to turn it into a stressful golf lesson, focusing all too intently on my children's technique and swing and grip … and I've never actually been *real* golfing! Somehow I couldn't just let us play; I had to bring precision and rules and structure to something that is intended to be completely wacky and unpredictable. Now when I'm trying to turn play into work, and adding unnecessary complication to something simple, I repeat the mantra "It's Just Mini-Golf."

Sitting WITH YOUR CHILD

Depending on the age of your child, you can invite her to sit in meditation with you. You may want to start with just 2–3 minutes if she's never tried meditation before. A sweet way to do this is to have her sit on your lap, with her back against your chest. Tell her that you are going to sit for a few minutes and breathe together, just noticing how our bodies feel when we breathe. If she has trouble following her own breath, she can pay attention to the sensations of your breath as she leans against you.

Mindful SNACK TIME

You can practice mindful eating with your children during snack time. This can work with any kind of food, but is usually best with something like raisins or chocolate that can be chewed or savored for a little while. First spend some time noticing what the food looks like and smells like, because usually we just pop it into our mouth without even seeing the food! Then see if there's a desire to gobble up the snack right away, instead of taking your time. Invite your child to place the food in her mouth, and see if you can make the raisin or chocolate last for an entire minute! (It helps to set a timer.) When you finish, talk about what it was like to eat slowly: Did it taste different? Did it feel different?

MANTRA

I CAN BE KIND TO SOMEONE ELSE TODAY.

I Spy

This is a fun activity to do with your child. Put on your top-secret spy senses, and see if you can spy …

- 5 things you can see right now
- 4 sounds you can hear right now
- 3 smells you can detect right now
- 2 sensations you can feel right now
- 1 thing you can taste right now.

MINDFUL Dinnertime

Try having a mindful family dinner. Each person can share what they are thankful for, and then you can eat your meal together mindfully. Talk about where the food came from and all the work that went into getting this meal to your table. See if everyone can eat in silence for the first three minutes, and then talk about what you notice when you eat slowly and mindfully. You could finish with a special dessert eaten in silence, and truly savor the sweetness.

Rainbow MEDITATION

Hone your mindful observation skills—and your child's—by seeing how quickly you can find every color in the rainbow in the space around you right now. This is an excellent game to engage your children while you're driving in the car.

CAN YOU *Help Me* UNDERSTAND?

This is a great question to ask your child when she is overwhelmed, misbehaving, or otherwise losing control over her actions. "Can you help me understand?" conveys a genuine desire to know what she's experiencing, and it helps her attempt to understand her own emotions. It allows her a moment to stop and reflect—and it gives you a moment to pause.

EMOTION *Charades*

To help kids understand how our emotions live in our bodies and express themselves through our faces and actions, you can play Emotion Charades. It's quite simple: someone acts out an emotion in complete silence, using posture, facial expressions, and movements. And everyone tries to guess what the emotion is. If you'd like, you can also engage your children in conversation about where in their bodies they feel that emotion, and what it feels like.

ROLLER-COASTER *Breathing*

Lie down on the floor with your child and place a cuddly toy on her belly. Tell her to imagine that she is going to give this creature the slowest roller-coaster ride imaginable. As she slowly breathes in and fills her belly, the toy will gently rise. Tell her that because the toy might get scared going down the roller-coaster at full speed, she needs to breathe out as slowly as possible, allowing it a soft ride down. And then repeat. This is a helpful way to teach slow belly breathing to your kids, and is a great practice for bedtime.

Techy MINDFULNESS WITH YOUR TEEN

Teens probably don't want to play mindfulness games, but that doesn't mean they couldn't use some mindfulness. You can introduce your teen to mindfulness through apps designed especially for him, such as "Stop, Breathe, and Think," or "Smiling Mind." If your teen is up for it, you could do the guided meditations in the app together.

Hard AND Soft

This is a good practice when you or your kids are feeling tense or stressed. Have everyone stand up, and reach their arms above their heads. Then instruct them to tighten their hands into fists, then (still keeping their hands in fists) squeeze all the muscles in their arms, then tense up their face, shoulders, stomach, back, legs. Ask them to make their entire body as tight as it can be, hold it, and then let everything go suddenly soft. (Repeat if that felt good.) Sometimes, it's easier to understand what it feels like to be relaxed if we first make everything tense, and then notice the contrast.

MANTRA

HOW CAN I BE KIND TO MYSELF TODAY?

LET IT Go

Just like us, our kids get anxious. A fun way to let the worries go is to actually let them go! Encourage your child to write down (or draw, for younger kids) her worries, and then let them go—rip them up, recycle them, make them into paper airplanes, burn them in a (safe, adult-supervised) bonfire, or keep them in a "worry box." Just giving voice to their worries helps kids process them (this might lead to some helpful conversations), and letting them go allows them to understand that thoughts and worries are not a permanent part of them—they're just thoughts.

Monkey MIND

Teach your kids about their "monkey mind," jumping from thought to thought the way a monkey swings from branch to branch, by having them pretend to be a monkey. Everyone playing stands in a circle. Instruct everyone to bring their attention to their breath. As soon as someone notices a thought, they "swing" like a monkey and move somewhere else in the room (they can also say their thought out loud if they'd like). This is a fun way to see that we all have thoughts (often quite random ones) all the time, but the important thing is to *notice* them.

MINDFULNESS IS *an Invitation*

Mindfulness is not something we want to force upon our children—if they are not interested in learning it, respect their wishes and wait until they are ready. Mindfulness practice should be an enjoyable activity that you can do together, not something children feel pressured to do, and it certainly shouldn't be used as a punishment or "time-out" technique. Take a moment to check your own intentions around teaching mindfulness to your kids. Are you offering a genuine invitation to learn something new, or are you trying to change their behavior in hopes of a particular outcome? If it's the latter, see if you can approach *teaching* mindfulness the way you approach *practicing* mindfulness: with curiosity, and without attachment to the results.

Quality TIME

The phrase "quality time" brings to mind the adage, "It's not quantity, it's quality." But many mothers still get hung up on the quantity part of the equation. We can't spend every single moment with our children, but we create quality time *when we are present for every single moment that we do spend with them.* Even if you have just a few minutes with your child, take a deep breath, and allow the to-do list to recede to the periphery of your awareness (it will be there when you're ready, believe me). Bring your attention to your body, to your surroundings, to your child's words, and *show up* for your time together.

Eye TO *Eye*

Together time is much richer with eye contact. Today, practice getting down to your child's level and making eye contact with him when you speak. This is incredibly effective when disciplining or correcting your child, and downright heart-melting when you're offering loving and encouraging words.

Sharing YOUR FEELINGS

If you're having a rough day, you can tell your child. It's hard for children to read our emotions, so honestly telling them what we're feeling (as appropriate for their age) can open up greater understanding. Let your child know that you're tired, or upset about something at work, or feeling like you're getting sick, and ask her if she ever feels that way. This helps your child develop empathy, and may improve your interactions on a difficult day.

A MINDFUL *Weekend*

It's easy to fill your weekend with classes and activities and outings. Can you leave a weekend completely unscheduled, and just do what everyone feels like when the weekend arrives? If it's been a rough week and everyone wants to stay in their jammies and watch movies, go with it. If you've been cooped up for a few rainy days and everyone wants to get out, go outside and play! What would it be like just to be in the moment and do what feels natural for a whole weekend?

THE CALM-DOWN CORNER

Create a calm-down corner or quiet space in your home. Have your children help you find soothing objects that you can keep there—blankets, stuffed animals, a bell or chime, sensory toys, or a favorite picture. Whenever your child feels overwhelmed, she can go to the calm-down corner and use one of her mindfulness practices, or simply snuggle with a blanket. This can be a great alternative to a time-out because it creates a space where your child can actively soothe herself. It also empowers her to look after her own feelings and needs.

CHAPTER 7

Savor

MINDFUL APPRECIATION

Our brains have what psychologists call a "negativity bias," which means we pay more attention to negative events than positive ones. This serves an evolutionary purpose, because it means we're attentive to danger, but sadly it also means we miss out on a lot of the small, ordinary joys. In this chapter, you'll learn practices that will help you pay more attention to the good (which is really good for you), and how to savor the fleeting moments of beauty that make motherhood so incredibly powerful.

A *Mindful* JAR

Each day, take a small piece of paper and write down one experience you had of being mindful during the day (a time you were fully present, a moment you truly appreciated, a freak-out you managed to soothe with your breath). Put this paper in a Mindful Jar (a simple canning jar will work), and after a few weeks and months you'll have a lovely collection of savored moments.

MANTRA

I WILL FULLY EXPERIENCE THIS GOOD FEELING.

Hugging MEDITATION

Pay attention to the hugs today. What does it feel like to have your arms around your child, his arms around you? Does he hold you tightly or softly, does he hug quickly or does he linger? What emotions and thoughts arise when you embrace? Can you truly be here, in this hug, and keep it with you all day?

Pay Attention
TO THIS MOMENT

Since moments are so … momentary … we may think that any individual moment isn't all that important. But what's in a moment? A breath, a thought, a memory, a worry, a smile, a sneeze. A sip of water, a twinge in your knee, a cry from the other room, a bug on the wall, a breeze just outside, a dog barking, a car in the distance. The hum of the lights, a creak in the floor, the air conditioner kicking in, the buzzing of your phone. What's in a moment? Just everything.

HEAR HER *Sing*

The next time you hear your child singing, pause and really listen, as if you're taking a mental recording. Notice the words and tones and vibrations her body is producing. Take a moment to appreciate the innocent and vulnerable high-pitched sound of a child's voice. Hear how she pronounces the words, and see if she makes up her own lyrics. Let the melody she sings linger in your awareness.

Smile

Research shows that smiling makes you feel happier. Take a deep breath in, and on the exhale, bring your lips into a slight smile (think more "Mona Lisa" and less "say cheese!") Hold your gentle smile for a few seconds, and notice how it feels.

Mindful CARPOOL

Like many mothers, you may spend a lot of time driving kids from one activity to the next. If you are playing chauffeur today, see if you can use that time to connect with your child and her friends: talk about their activities, sing together to a fun song on the radio, or play a classic car game, such as "I spy."

I HELPED MAKE THIS
Amazing Moment HAPPEN

When things *do* go exactly as you planned, and your child is in good spirits and you share a meaningful experience together, don't just chalk it up to chance. You participated in making it happen. You supported your child with your loving presence and attention, and all of your actions in previous moments led to this beautiful moment. Acknowledge your special contribution to making this amazing moment happen.

TOTALLY *Awesome!*

When we experience awe, we feel good. Awe is a sense of being part of something bigger than ourselves, or an experience of having to adjust and expand our thinking to accommodate unexpected information. We generally experience awe when we 1) are outdoors, or 2) witness unexpected kind acts. So take some time to step outside today and admire the big, beautiful world: the vast sky above your home and the steady trees in your yard. And when you see an act of kindness today, such as a sweet and tender moment between your children, soak it in and experience the awesome.

MANTRA

I WILL

BE

PRESENT

FOR THIS

SPECIAL

AND

PRECIOUS

MOMENT.

LITTLE *Laughs*

Laughter is joy made audible. When your child laughs today, soak it in. Notice the smile, the light, the joy, the ease in your child's face. Let the sound ring in your ears. Join him in his joy.

Tender KISSES

If you get a kiss from your child today, savor this expression of love. Notice if her kiss is gentle or full of pressure, if it's big or small, if it's loud or quiet. Inhale the sweet smell of her skin and hair. Can you feel or hear her heartbeat? Check in with what it feels like to receive this act of tenderness and care from your child.

WHEN WE *Cling* TO THE *Good*

With mindfulness, we come to realize that all of our difficult moments will ultimately pass. And that means our good moments will eventually come to an end, too. The secret to truly living and loving those moments is to not cling to them. Sometimes we hold those experiences so tightly, fearing they may never come again, that we almost crush them. We don't even really enjoy them because we're so worried that they'll end. They *will* end, as all moments do. When we don't frantically cling to the good, and relax into it instead, it expands and nourishes us.

Visual REST

Your eyes take in so much information and stimulation throughout the day—and they need a break. Take a minute to close your eyes and notice what it feels like to give your vision a rest.

MY CHILD IS *Amazing*

Start a page in your journal that's titled "My child is amazing because …" and write down all the beautiful and wonderful and unique and human and silly and profound things that make your child amazing. Add to it when you can, and keep it handy, so you can look at it during the not-so-amazing moments.

Safe PLACE

Where are the places in your body where you generally feel good and safe? Where do you *not* tend to carry a lot of emotion and tension? For most people, these safe places in the body are near the extremities—the hands, the knees, the feet. Our difficult emotions tend to be felt in the gut or the chest, so spend some time savoring the sensations in the parts of the body that feel safe.

THIS IS WHAT *Calm* FEELS LIKE

Today, bring special attention to the moments when you feel calm. It's easy to miss them because they're so, well, calm. When you notice that your body is at rest, your muscles are relaxed, and your heart rate and breathing are slow, simply note, "This is what calm feels like." Spend a few moments savoring—and remembering—the calm. Know that you can call upon this feeling of calm at any moment of your day.

Savor THE SWEET

We often overlook the small moments of goodness and sweetness in our midst (which is a good thing for our physical survival, but not so good for our mental health). Research shows that we need to spend about 20 seconds with a positive experience to make it "stick." Today, set an intention to savor the sweet. When your child gives you a hug, or makes you laugh, take a deep breath and be fully in that moment. Notice how it feels when you are happy and joyful. Savor the sweet.

MAKE A *Happy List*

Make a list of the things that make you feel happy. What is it that brings you joy? What makes you feel safe? When do you feel a sense of *enough*, a sense of not-wanting? Post your list where you can see it—continue to add to it, allow it to inspire you, and, if it makes you happy, smile whenever you walk past it.

Camera Roll MEDITATION

Take a few moments to scroll through the camera roll on your phone. Spend some time appreciating your smiling children, revisiting a happy memory, and marveling at how much of your beautiful life is captured (and how much is *not* captured) on this little device.

One Word JOURNAL

Keep a small journal in which you write down ONE WORD each day. It could be a word to describe yourself and how you felt, your child, or your entire day. Perhaps you could describe your busy day as "full," or simply note that the day was "exhilarating," "challenging," "overwhelming," or "exciting." After a few weeks and months, you'll have a vivid portrayal of how much your experience, for yourself and your child, can vary from day to day.

MANTRA

I HAVE SO MUCH TO BE THANKFUL FOR.

Joy

Joy can be found in any moment of your day. Happiness is fleeting, and is often tied to specific circumstances, but joy is enduring. Joy can be about finding the space between wanting and not-wanting, between pushing and pulling. You can find joy in the simple rest between two deep breaths. Joy can be a peaceful acceptance of every moment.

MUSIC *Meditation*

Put on some music you like and pay attention to how you feel as you listen. What do you notice in your body? What thoughts arise? Does the music make you feel calm, energized, or something else? Savor the power music has to awaken so many emotions, memories, thoughts, sensations, and experiences.

COME *Alive*

What makes you feel *alive*? What do you do that truly energizes you, that awakens a sense of empowerment and vitality? It might be dancing, running, walking, cooking, crafting … anything that you experience with mind and body and leaves you feeling strong and invigorated. Whatever it is, make some time for it today.

Equanimity

I think equanimity is the most beautiful—and important—concept in mindfulness. "Equanimity" literally means "equal strength," but it's sometimes referred to as "non-interfering." With mindfulness, we have the strength to be in the middle of some pretty strong forces—love and hurt, joy and anger, beauty and boredom. We have the strength to meet our experience without clinging or pushing, without trying to make it anything other than what it is. It's a way of standing in the middle of everything with courageous power, not passive resignation. It's a dynamic way of being in the world with presence. It is absolutely life-changing to approach our daily experiences with equanimity.

MINDFUL *Journaling*

Journaling may be one of the best forms of therapy. It's a great way to connect with yourself and your emotions, and can help you understand what you feel and who you are. Spend a few moments each day writing. Don't worry about structure and grammar—this is just for you. You could even set a timer for 5 minutes and just free-write. Many writers have said that they don't really know what they think until they write it down. Journaling can be a powerful part of your mindfulness practice, as you become more familiar with your thoughts. You can use your journal as a place to "dump" your thoughts without having to return to them, or you can use it to reflect on your growth or to sort out your thoughts about a difficult situation.

NOTHING *Special* IS HAPPENING

Meditation can sometimes seem boring. But the beauty of meditation is that when nothing special is happening, something special *is* happening. You are breathing. You are alive. You are completely awake and present to your experience. That is incredibly special.

"*Today* I WILL NOTICE"

Set an intention to *notice* today. Perhaps you want to notice acts of generosity, things that are beautiful, kindly spoken words, or freely given smiles. When we intentionally look for things, we're much more likely to see them, and we can remind ourselves that goodness is always waiting to be discovered.

MANTRA

I WILL LOOK FOR THE GOOD.

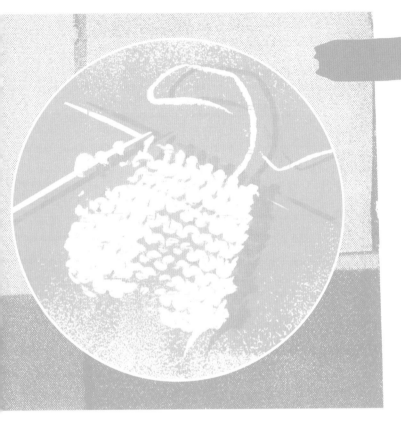

Flow

Psychologist Mihaly Csikszentmihalyi tells us that one of the most positive mental experiences we can have is a state of *flow*. We usually achieve flow when we're doing a challenging and enjoyable activity that matches, or is just above, our ability level, and we're doing it purely for the sake of the activity itself. We focus on our task with a single-pointed concentration, and things just … flow. What activities create a flow state for you? It might be reading, knitting, gardening, sewing, coloring, or any number of endeavors. Take some time to explore the things that allow you to flow, and then do them, frequently and joyfully.

FEEL *Gratitude*

When something powerful or amazing happens, we often describe being "moved" or "touched": it's a *physical* experience. Spend some time today reflecting on the good things in your life that you are thankful for, and notice how it feels in the body when you cultivate joy and gratitude.

YOU'VE NEVER SEEN *Today*

Sure, you've seen Mondays, carpool days, holidays, sunny days, rainy days, school days, and laundry days before, but you've never seen today. Can you drop your expectations and stories about today? You may be just a few hours into today, but you've already decided "Today is *this*" or "Today is *that*." But you've never seen today. Can you keep your eyes—and mind—open?

Good Enough REASONS

In his book *Waking Up*, neuroscientist Sam Harris writes, "Most of us spend our time seeking happiness and security without acknowledging the underlying purpose of our search. Each of us is looking for a path back to the present: We are trying to find good enough reasons to be satisfied *now*." I love the line: "good enough reasons to be satisfied *now*." Life will never be perfect, so can you be satisfied? Can you look for the "good enough" today? Can you appreciate that "good enough" is pretty amazing?

Read A POEM

Read your favorite poem today. Read it out loud and notice the words that jump out at you. Pay attention to your body and how it feels as you read. Savor the power that someone else's words can have on your experience. (If you don't have a favorite poem, you can easily explore poetry online. Try reading Rumi's "The Guest House" or Portia Nelson's "Autobiography in Five Short Chapters" to get started.)

DAY *Dreaming*

You can't be 100 percent mindful and attentive 100 percent of the time … nor would you really want to be. Research shows that mind-wandering is actually good for us (provided we don't do it when we're driving or performing surgery). When the mind wanders, we often stumble upon solutions and creative ideas that our purpose-driven, thinking mind would never discover. Take a few quiet moments today just to let your mind wander, and see where it goes.

WHEN THE *Stars Align*

The good and ordinary moments can pass us by because they're just that—ordinary. But if today you happen to capture a moment when everyone—you, the kids, your partner, even the dog—is in a good mood and things feel harmonious and there's no crisis, stop and take it in. As far as I'm concerned, that's a "stars aligning" moment, and it is meant to be treasured and savored.

HOW WAS YOUR *Day at School?*

Mothers tell me this is one of their favorite times of the day—hearing about all that their child does at school. Today, spend some time after school being fully present with your child and asking about her day: What did she learn? What was fun? Who did she talk to? Did anything silly happen? What was hard? Was anything surprising? If your child answers simply, "It was fine," or "Nothing happened," you can ask a more specific question—"Can you tell me three things you learned?" or "Can you think of one way today was different from yesterday?" You could also tell her about your day, or what your favorite part of the day was, and see if that encourages her to talk about her experiences.

WHAT DOES IT FEEL LIKE *Not* TO BE ANGRY?

Today, bring your attention to the times you are *not* angry. Even if you are usually easily angered, you may be surprised at how much of your day you are not upset or irritated. When you notice these moments, take comfort in them: What does it feel like in your body? What thoughts are you having? What's it like *not* to be angry?

EXPAND YOUR *Worldview*

Seek out opportunities to expand your worldview and see things from a new perspective. Read a book, listen to a podcast, or watch a documentary on something that is unfamiliar to you. Savor the experience of learning something new.

BE *Pollyanna* FOR A MOMENT

Trust me, I know that not everything in life is unicorns and rainbows, but I also know that there is great power (even unicorn-and-rainbow-like magic!) in the ability to take something difficult and find the good in it. If you're struggling with potty-training your preschooler, can you be grateful for running water and washing machines? If your daughter is in a particularly sassy phase, can you appreciate her spirit and independence?

INVITE *Laughter*

What makes you laugh? Whatever it is, seek it out today. Watch silly cat videos, read a good book, watch your favorite comedy, tell jokes with your kids, or play a physical game such as charades. Laughing is probably the most fun way to breathe … so get your silly on today and make that your mindfulness practice.

MANTRA

MAY I SEE BEAUTY IN EVERYTHING.

DO *Some* GOOD

Find a way to do some good in your part of the world—volunteer, donate items to a local charity, or clean up the neighborhood park. If your kids are old enough, invite them to join you and enjoy the feeling of playing a part in your community.

Connect WITH NATURE

Our modern lives disconnect us from a basic part of our nature, which is connecting with nature! Get outside today and let your bare feet touch the earth, feel the wind on your face, take in the smell of the outdoors, and listen to the sounds of the world around you. In the summer months, you could even consider doing your daily mindfulness and meditation practice outdoors.

Sing!

When you sing, you take a short inhalation, and then let the words out with a long exhalation. It's a musical form of belly breathing! Even if it's just in the shower, or by yourself in the car, channel your inner diva and belt out some tunes today.

CHAPTER 8

Close of Day

EVENING PRACTICES

Today you had an invitation—to show up, to make mistakes, to make amends, and to pay attention. Tonight is a time to invite rest and reflection. It is a time to be compassionate with yourself for your mistakes, to commit to new intentions for tomorrow, and to nurture yourself with loving care and restorative sleep. In this chapter, you'll find practices for closing your day with presence, stillness, and love.

THE *Good*, THE *Difficult*, AND THE *Helpful*

Take time out at the end of the day to sit down with your children and reflect on what was good today, what was hard today, and who you helped today (or who helped you)? Take turns to share this information. It's a lovely way to take a balanced look at the day, and to remind ourselves about how we want to interact with others.

WHEN YOU *Lose It* AT THE END OF THE DAY

You've had your mindful mojo with you all day, handling conflicts with ease and keeping your cool, even when the kiddos were totally fired up. You met moment after moment with presence and compassion. And then … all those expenditures of self-control took their toll and you lost it. Maybe you yelled, maybe you said something you now wish you hadn't. It's easy to feel like the day is a disaster when, after being triggered for the 31st time, you just couldn't do "the pause and breathe thing" again. But guess what? You kept your cool and *didn't* lose it *30 times* before that! And that's amazing. Make amends with your child, and honor yourself for the difficult work you're doing, Mama.

MANTRA

I DID
MY BEST
TODAY.

Bedtime MEDITATION

When my children were infants,
rocking them to sleep at night
became a meditation. I knew
that once their eyes closed, if
I counted to 100 they would stay
asleep when I put them down in
their crib. I would begin counting
in time to my rocking, which
started to match the rhythm of
my breath. Staring at a sweet
sleeping face, the numbers in my
head became a mantra, tethering
me to the present moment and
allowing me to savor the end of
this day with my child.

Tomorrow I WILL DO BETTER

We all have rough days. We all have days when we yell, when we lose it, when we're
not present, when we're not the mother we want to be. When you have one of those
days, take a deep breath. Place your hand on your heart and remind yourself that you
did the best you could with the resources (time, energy, sanity) that you had today.
On the in-breath, send yourself some kindness and compassion. On the out-breath,
remember that tomorrow is a chance to begin again. Tomorrow, you will do better.

MANTRA

I WELCOME,
AND SAVOR,
REST.

SLEEPING *Beauty*

Before you go to bed, check in on your sleeping child. Notice how relaxed his face and body are, observe the gentle rise and fall of his chest, and listen to the soft sounds of his breath. Place your hand on your heart and notice how *your* body feels as you watch your child in sweet repose. This tender image of your sleeping child can be called upon at any moment of your day when you need to remind yourself of the innate goodness and sweetness of your little one.

Gratitude BODY SCAN

When you lie down in bed tonight, take 5 minutes to close your eyes and gently scan your body. Begin with your feet, noticing any sensations that are present—warmth or coolness, aching or pressure. If you don't notice any obvious sensations, just note that. Take a moment to express gratitude for all the running and walking and standing your feet allowed you to do today.

Then proceed to your legs, noticing any sensations and holding gratitude for all that your lower limbs did today—sitting on the floor, bouncing your child, crawling around the house. With another full breath, notice your torso, chest, and arms, thanking them for all the hug-giving, tear-wiping, and deep breathing throughout the day. Finally, bring your attention to your face and head, fully appreciating all the smiles and words and kisses you engaged in today. Take a few more deep breaths, with gratitude for your body and with deep respect for the embodied nature of motherhood.

Five GOOD THINGS

Before you go to bed, list five good things that happened today. You can do this in a journal, or simply tick them off on your fingers. Even the smallest win ("I separated two Legos without breaking a nail") counts!

MANTRA

I GIVE MYSELF PERMISSION TO NO LONGER BE ON THE GO.

WHAT *Moved* YOU TODAY?

Did your four-year-old drop a truth-bomb? Did you get a sweet and unexpected hug from your teen? Did a wave of deep love or empathy swell up and surprise you? Did you witness a kind act between your children, or by a stranger? Did you get a misspelled and grammatically incorrect love note from your first-grader? Did you have a moment of presence and awareness and connection? What moved you today?

Sit With YOUR PARTNER

If you have a partner in parenting, ask if the two of you could sit in silence together for a few moments tonight. Sitting and breathing together, you may notice that your breath begins to synchronize as you attune to each other's presence. You can continue to be in silence, or share kind words of gratitude and appreciation.

Middle of the Night MEDITATION

When your child wakes you in the middle of the night, it's often for a desperate need: she's likely hungry, frightened, or sick. The darkness and stillness of night make it easier to shut out the world and focus entirely on your current task: providing comfort to and nurturing your child, even in a bleary-eyed and sleepy state. This nighttime parenting can be an act of mindful meditation, as you hold your child close, whisper soothing words in her ear, and begin to bring your breathing into alignment with hers. You may wish you were still in bed sleeping, but see if you can relax as much as possible into this tender twilight moment.

PREPARE FOR *Tomorrow*

You probably have routines for readying the house and the kids for the next morning—selecting outfits, packing lunches, organizing backpacks. Save a few moments to prepare yourself *mentally* for tomorrow. What will be needed of you? What do *you* need? Will you be facing a difficult situation that demands some extra self-compassion or self-care? Spend a few moments tonight preparing yourself for your encounter with tomorrow.

Sunset MEDITATION

For one week, see if you can watch the sun set each night (this might be fun to do with your kids). What is different about each sunset, and what is the same? What's different about *you* each night, and what is the same? Allow the sunset to be a time to greet the end of the day and transition into rest.

BEDROOM *Retreat*

As it's often the last place you tidy up, take some time today to make your bedroom a nurturing space to retreat to at the end of the day: diffuse some lavender essential oil, light a candle, fluff up your pillows, add a fuzzy blanket to your bed, get a heating pad or hot-water bottle, or just clear out the clutter so you can truly relax at the end of your day.

Silent NIGHT

As mothers, we rarely experience silence. Tonight, after the kids go to bed, institute a silent night: no TV, no chores, no email, no catching up on work, no conversation, just silence. Turn down the lights, enjoy a soothing beverage, and savor the quiet solitude.

Yawn

Go ahead and give in to that yawn at the end of the day. When you pay attention to your yawn, you may realize just how good it feels—it activates the soothing part of your nervous system, releases oxytocin and serotonin, which are feel-good hormones, and helps you feel more relaxed. In fact, just reading this probably makes you want to yawn ... so go ahead.

MANTRA

TOMORROW IS A CHANCE FOR ME TO BEGIN AGAIN.

WHEN YOU *Can't Sleep*

In the *Book of Joy*, the Dalai Lama shares his trick for insomnia: When he can't sleep, he thinks of all the other people throughout the world that, right at that moment, also cannot fall asleep. If you're awake in the wee hours of the night, you can be sure a lot of other mothers are also up nursing, tossing and turning, or tending to their children. Being awake in the middle of the night can feel profoundly isolating; see if you can find comfort in knowing that as a sleepless mother, you are not alone.

Night Sky MEDITATION

Before you go to bed tonight, step outside and look up at the night sky. Whether you see just a few stars or an entire galaxy, take a moment to remind yourself that you are stardust. You and the stars and your kids and all the other mothers are all made from the same shining universe stuff. You're all in this together, and you, yes *you*, are a star.

SLEEP AS *Surrender*

As you climb into bed tonight, remember that sleep is a powerful lesson in surrender: we don't know when and how we will slide from wakefulness into slumber, but we know it will happen. All we can do is create the proper conditions, and then lie down and trust.

SLEEP *Meditation*

Before you go to sleep, remember to SLEEP:

Savor: What's one positive thing you want to remember about today?

Learn: What's one thing you learned from today?

Ease: What can you do to bring ease to tomorrow?

Engage: What can you do to bring energy to tomorrow?

Prepare: What do you need to do to be ready for tomorrow?

MANTRA

TODAY
WAS HARD.
BUT I
DID IT.
AND I AM
STRONGER
FOR IT.

BEDTIME *Massage*

Give your hard-working body a bit of love before bed—rub some lotion or essential oils on your hands and feet, massage your temples and cheeks and jaw, and gently tend to any aching muscles. Place a warm lavender compress on your forehead, snuggle up to a heating pad, and take a few soothing deep breaths.

Your Mindful Life

With mindfulness, we accept whatever is present.
Because that's WHAT IS.

It's not resignation—it's simply recognizing this is what
it's like right now.

And then we have a choice.

If it's something we can change, we can work in the next
moment to change it.

If it's something we cannot change, we can choose to
soften into it.

Mindfulness doesn't eliminate the stressors from your life.
Your children will still throw tantrums, people will still cut
you off in traffic, and it may rain sometimes.

The profound transformation takes place within you.
You choose to relate to the stressors in life more skillfully.

And that is LIFE-CHANGING.

YOU'VE GOT THIS, MAMA.

Resources

WEBSITES

Left Brain Buddha: The Modern Mindful Life
www.leftbrainbuddha.com
Author's blog.

Mindful Parenting
blogs.psychcentral.com/
mindful-parenting
Blog by Carla Naumburg, Ph.D., at Psych Central.

Dr Dan Siegel
www.drdansiegel.com
Resources on mindfulness.

Greater Good Science Center
greatergood.berkeley.edu/
mindfulness
Articles and more.

Be Mindful
www.bemindful.co.uk
Search for courses on mindfulness near you in the UK.

Centre for Mindfulness Practice and Research UK
www.bangor.ac.uk/mindfulness
Updates on the latest research, including mindful parenting.

The Mindful Parenting & Community Project
www.connectingwithmindfulness.co.uk
Mindful parenting courses in Bristol, UK.

APPS

All the apps listed below are available for iOS and Android.

For mothers:
Headspace
10% Happier
Insight Timer
Calm

For kids:
Stop, Breathe, & Think
Smiling Mind
Breathe Think Do with Sesame
Settle Your Glitter

BOOKS

Everyday Blessings: The Inner Work of Mindful Parenting by Myla and Jon Kabat-Zinn, Hachette, 1998

The Mindful Child: How to Help Your Kid Manage Stress and Become Happier, Kinder, and More Compassionate by Susan Kaiser Greenland, Atria Books, 2010

Parenting in the Present Moment by Carla Naumburg, Ph.D, Parallax Press, 2014

Ready, Set, Breathe: Practicing Mindfulness with Your Children for Fewer Meltdowns and a More Peaceful Family by Carla Naumburg, Ph.D, New Harbinger Publications, 2015

The Whole-Brain Child: 12 Revolutionary Strategies to Nurture Your Child's Developing Mind by Daniel J. Siegel, M.D., and Tina Payne Bryson, Ph.D., Bantam, 2012

Brainstorm: The Power and Purpose of the Teenage Brain by Daniel J. Siegel, M.D., TarcherPerigee, 2014

Sitting Still Like a Frog: Mindfulness Exercises for Kids (and Their Parents) by Eline Snel, Shambhala, 2013

Planting Seeds: Practicing Mindfulness with Children by Thich Nhat Hanh and the Plum Village Community, Parallax Press, 2007

Index

Acknowledgments

Thank you to the team at CICO Books and Ryland Peters & Small for their vision for this book and their support and guidance through the process of bringing it to life: Cindy Richards, Carmel Edmonds, Kristine Pidkameny, and Dawn Bates. A special thank you to Clare Nicholas for the gorgeous illustrations and to Abigail Read for the soothing designs that convey such a sense of peace and calm throughout the book.

This book is the product of two deeply intertwined paths in my life: motherhood and mindfulness. I have been incredibly fortunate to have skilled and supportive guides along both these journeys.

I am indebted to the many wonderful teachers who have helped me deepen my understanding of mindfulness and supported me in my practice, especially the amazing team at Mindful Schools: Megan Cowan, Chris McKenna, Vinny Ferraro, Pam Dunn, and Christina Costelo. Thank you to Marc Anderson for your continued mentorship, guidance, and friendship. I also owe a debt of gratitude to the teachers whom I have never met, but whose words have inspired my practice: Jon Kabat-Zinn, Daniel J. Siegel, Tara Brach, Joseph Goldstein, Sam Harris, Brené Brown, Chade-Meng Tan, Rick Hanson, Stephen Porges, and Peter A. Levine.

I am incredibly humbled by the support and encouragement from my readers at Left Brain Buddha, who have inspired me to speak honestly about motherhood and about my struggles and joys, for I have discovered that they are *your* struggles and joys, too.

Thank you to my friends who have supported me as a mother, teacher, writer, and human, and promised me that I would indeed write a book one day. Tera and Christy, thank you for all your magic-making! Amber, I can't imagine being a mother without my sister—thanks for not judging my less-than-mindful-mama moments, and helping me keep my sense of humor.

I am deeply grateful for *my* mother, Lynn Rudell: you are loving and generous and brilliant, and, in partnership with the equally loving and generous and brilliant Bob Rudell, you have given me the greatest gift … a beautiful childhood and an exquisite model of perfectly imperfect parenting. Thank you both for helping me become the mother, and the person, that I am today.

Finally, I am deeply grateful to my husband and children for, well, pretty much everything. Todd, thank you for being my partner in this crazy adventure. Abby and Liam, thank you for the laughter and light and joy you bring to our life together. My heart just bursts with love for all of you.